CLASSIC AMERICAN WRITERS

Willa Cather

ANN T. KEENE

Julian Ⓜ Messner
Published by Simon & Schuster
New York   London   Toronto   Sydney   Tokyo   Singapore

For Mary Comegys,
Genevieve Larmouth,
Pauline Peirce, and
Juanita Schoff—
four special teachers.

JULIAN MESSNER
Published by Simon & Schuster
1230 Avenue of the Americas
New York, NY 10020.

Manufactured in the United States of America
Book design by Virginia Pope.

10 9 8 7 6 5 4 3 2 1

Library of Congress Cataloging-in-Publication Data
Keene, Ann T.
    Willa Cather / by Ann T. Keene.
        p.   cm. — (Classic American writers)
    Includes bibliographical references and index.
    1. Cather, Willa, 1873-1947—Biography—Juvenile literature.
2. Women novelists, American—20th century—Biography—Juvenile
literature.   [1. Cather, Willa, 1873–1947.   2. Authors, American.
3. Women—Biography.]   I. Title.   II. Series.
PS3505.A87Z686   1994   813'.52—dc20   [B]   93-45743   CIP   AC
ISBN 0-671-86760-1

CONTENTS

Willa Cather's birthplace (above), Grandmother Boak's farmhouse in Back Creek Valley, Virginia, and her first home (below), Willow Shade.

ONE

Beginning
a Journey

The years from eight to fifteen are the formative period of a writer's life, when he unconsciously gathers basic material. He may acquire a great many interesting and vivid impressions in his mature years but his thematic material he acquires under fifteen years of age.[1]　　　　　—Willa Cather

On a cold day in late March 1883, at the small depot in Back Creek Valley, Virginia, a group of eleven people gathered to board a Burlington Railroad train. Their ultimate destination was a farming settlement near Red Cloud, Nebraska, more than a thousand miles to the west. Heading the group was Charles Cather, a sheep farmer, who was moving his wife, their four children, and other relatives to a new life on the prairie. A few months earlier his barn had burned to the ground, and Cather had decided it was time to start over.

In choosing to homestead in the West, Charles Cather was something of a latecomer. In the nearly two decades following the Civil War, hundreds of thousands of easterners—both longtime residents and recently arrived immigrants—had already preceded him. Encouraging this massive migration were the newly established railroads, which had received large tracts of land from the U.S. government as an incentive to extend their routes. In turn, the railroad companies encouraged settlement along the lines by offering acreage at low prices.

To raise money for the trip, Charles Cather had auctioned off his house, furniture, and farming equipment for $6,000. The remaining possessions of the family—their clothing and books, china and silver—were stowed in boxes and barrels to make the long train journey. Belongings that could not be packed had to be left behind—like Vic, the loyal family sheep-dog, who had been given to a neighbor.

Vic was especially dear to the oldest Cather child, a nine-year-old girl who had been christened Wilella, in memory of a deceased aunt, and whom everyone called Willie. Vic and Willie had been inseparable companions, roaming the woods and fields near their rural home, Willow Shade. Because Willie worried about Vic's feet as she herded sheep along sharp, rocky roads, kindly Mr. Cather made little leather shoes for Vic and the other farm dogs to wear.

Willie loved Willow Shade, and she was nervous about the new life that lay ahead. Her parents tried to reassure her by pointing out that relatives would be there to greet them. Her father's brother, her uncle George, and his wife, Frances, had moved to south-central Nebraska a decade earlier. They had been joined a few years later by her grandparents William and Caroline Cather.

The Nebraska Cathers had written glowing accounts of their lives on the Divide, a broad strip of prairie between the Little Blue and the Republican rivers. They found the dry climate especially appealing, and believed that it was healthier than their homeland, the damp Shenandoah Valley of northern Virginia that harbored serious illnesses, especially tuberculosis.

Willie's family had roots in Virginia extending back more than a century. The first Cather in America had been her great-great-grandfather Jasper, a schoolteacher who had emigrated from Northern Ireland in the mid-1700s. Jasper Cather settled in western Pennsylvania and later fought in the Revolutionary

Charles Cather and Mary Virginia Boak Cather, parents of Willa Cather.
In middle age Cather recalled her earliest childhood memory: riding happily
in a sleigh through the snowy Virginia countryside, tucked securely under
blankets between her parents.

War. After the war he bought land in Frederick County, Virginia, married a local woman named Sarah Moore, and raised a family of seven children.

Jasper Cather's descendants continued to farm in northern Virginia. In the late 1850s his grandson William—Willie's grandfather—had built Willow Shade in Back Creek Valley, near Winchester, as a home for himself and his wife, Caroline. After William and Caroline migrated to Nebraska in 1877, their son Charles and his family moved from their nearby home into Willow Shade.

Charles Cather had married Mary Virginia Boak, a childhood friend with Virginia roots as deep as her husband's, on December 5, 1872. Mary Virginia, nicknamed Jennie, had been a schoolteacher in Back Creek Valley before their marriage. A year later, on December 7, 1873, their first child, Wilella, was born at Grandmother Boak's house in Back Creek Valley.

Nearly a decade later, the Virginia chapter in the lives of

Willie and her family was drawing to a close. With great clouds of steam and the squawk of a raucous whistle, a passenger train pulled into the small country station. After their possessions were loaded into the baggage car, the Cather party climbed into the coach: Willie and her two excited younger brothers, Roscoe and Douglas; Mrs. Cather, carrying baby Jessica, assisted up the steep steps by her husband; Grandmother Rachel Boak, Mrs. Cather's mother; two of Mrs. Boak's grandchildren; and finally the hired girl, Margie Anderson, and her brother.

The doors closed, the whistle sounded, and the train began to move forward. Settling into her red plush seat, Willie glanced out the window—and saw Vic tearing across the field toward the train, dragging her chain. The old dog had broken loose in a last effort to be reunited with her family. Fighting tears, Willie turned away and forced herself to look straight ahead.

The Charles Cather party arrived in Red Cloud, Nebraska, a town of 1,200 inhabitants, on a sunny spring day in early April. At the train station they piled their belongings and themselves into several Studebaker farm wagons that would take them to "Catherton," the site of the family settlement a dozen miles to the northwest.

Willie settled in the hay near the side of the wagon box to steady herself as it bumped along the faint trail barely visible in the thick bunch grass. The land seemed strange and alien: treeless, and flat as far as the eye could see, "like sheet iron," she later recalled, with no sign of human habitation.[2]

As the wagons moved farther and farther into the country, Willie began to believe that she was coming "to the end of everything." She tried hard not to cry—her father had told her that pioneers needed "grit" to establish themselves on the prairies, and she did not want to disappoint him. When an occasional meadowlark flew near the wagons, however, its melancholy song somehow reminded her of all she had left behind and tears gathered in her eyes.[3]

Later that day the wagons delivered the Cather party and their belongings to the farmhouse of Willie's grandparents William and Caroline. Willie's anxiety and displeasure receded somewhat during the next few days as the group resettled themselves in their new home. Shortly after their arrival, William Cather returned to Virginia for an extended visit, and Caroline went to live with her son George on his own farm nearby. The newly arrived Cathers and those accompanying them now had the place to themselves.

Charles Cather soon established himself as a typical prairie farmer, raising corn and hogs. Jennie Cather devoted herself to the arduous life of a farm wife: she cooked, sewed, gardened—keeping a sharp eye out for rattlesnakes—preserved foods, looked after the children, and kept the frame house tidy with the help of Margie, the hired girl.

Young Willie's brightness and curiosity gradually overcame her displeasure at leaving her cherished home in Willow Shade as she became caught up in the daily routine of life on the Divide. She often ran errands for her parents, riding a pony that her father had given her. These included frequent trips to the post office—at a farm several miles away—to pick up the mail. In addition, there was school to attend—though only for three months at a time, in a simple wooden building that also served as Catherton's only church. The church sponsored a Sunday school that met weekly nine months of the year, and Willie was a member of its primary class, taught by Grandmother Cather.

Willie's formal education was supplemented at home by Grandmother Boak, who had begun teaching her at Willow Shade. Like many families from the East who had resettled in the West, the Cathers boasted a home library that included the plays and poems of Shakespeare, complete editions of the works of nineteenth-century English and American writers, and volumes of ancient and modern history. Selections from these books and from the Bible were regularly read aloud at family gatherings in the evening.

Weather permitting, Willie still had lots of free time to

explore the countryside. Sometimes she was accompanied by her younger brothers, Roscoe and Douglas, but she preferred to ride by herself over the flat prairie, seeking out small creeks where native cottonwood trees grew, or looking for "wallows," water-filled depressions made years before by trampling herds of buffalo. Trees and water on the prairie were always a delightful discovery. In the summer scattered sunflowers and coreopsis, another local flower, erupted in bursts of golden color. Her new home, she decided, might not be as appealing as Virginia, but it had a beauty all its own.

Not long after arriving on the Divide, the sociable Willie made friends with the Lambrechts, a family of German immigrants who lived on the adjoining farm, and the Lambrecht children became her first Nebraska playmates. In her rides on the prairie, she discovered other immigrant families—mostly Swedes, Danes, Norwegians, and Bohemians (former residents of what later became Czechoslovakia). In fact, the foreign-born population outnumbered American-born settlers by at least three to one.

Willie loved to visit in the households of these immigrant settlers and hear their different languages. She would sit for hours and keep the women company as they churned butter or sewed clothes or baked. Many of them spoke very little English, but she still managed to understand the stories they told her. She listened carefully as they related tales of life in the old country and in the new, years before her birth. She listened—and she remembered.

Just as Willie was settling into the routine of life on the Divide, her days there came to an end. By the summer of 1884, Charles Cather had decided to sell the farm and move into the town of Red Cloud.

There were several reasons for his decision. Rural life had not been easy for Jennie Cather, a ladylike woman who found the isolation hard to bear. The Cathers were also bothered by

the long distance that separated them from medical care: Jennie Cather had suffered at least one miscarriage during their
stay on the Divide, and Willie had been ill that year with a
mysterious disease—possibly a mild case of polio—that left
her temporarily lame. Most important of all, Charles and Jennie were bothered by the lack of adequate schooling for Willie,
who was obviously a very bright child, and her brothers
would soon need more education as well.

On September 11, 1884, Charles Cather advertised a public
sale of the farmhouse, land, livestock, and equipment. By the
end of the month the family was living in Red Cloud, and
Willie's father had opened an office to sell real estate and
insurance.

TWO

Red Cloud

Willie Cather was no stranger to Red Cloud, and many of its inhabitants knew who she was, too. The family had often come into town to buy domestic and farm supplies during their seventeen months at Catherton. During one such visit in 1883, Willie had been taken by her father to the local general store to buy a pair of shoes. Dressed in a smart-looking coat and matching hat made from fake leopardskin, she had regaled the store owner and other shoppers with a recitation on Shakespeare and English literary history, as well as an account of her life in Virginia.

A proud Charles Cather had no doubt prompted her, but the self-possessed little girl had amazed and impressed her audience. Soon after the family moved to town, she was giving recitations at public programs sponsored by the Sunday school at the Baptist church, which the Cather family attended. One of her favorite pieces was *The Song of Hiawatha*, a popular poem about a Native American written by Henry Wadsworth Longfellow; pretending to be the young Indian boy, she would recite excerpts from the poem wearing her fanciest dress and fashionably striped stockings, her long curls tied back with a ribbon—and carrying a bow and arrow.

Nine-year-old Wilella poses in the fashionable outfit she wore to recite "Hiawatha." Following a custom of the day, her cross was made from locks of her parents' hair.

Red Cloud had been founded in 1870 by a former Union Army officer, Silas Garber, who later became governor of Nebraska. The town was named after Chief Red Cloud of the Oglala tribe, who had become well-known following his trip to Washington, D.C., in 1870 to negotiate with the federal government on behalf of the Sioux Indians. Red Cloud was the seat, or government center, of Webster County. Its residents were mostly farmers, but there were also professional people—merchants, bankers, ministers, doctors, teachers, lawyers—as well as laborers and servants.

Indians had once challenged the settlement of whites in Nebraska, but by the 1880s they were no longer a threat to residents in the vicinity of Red Cloud. Many Native American hunting parties still passed through the area in search of buffalo, elk, and deer. There were other visitors to Red Cloud, too: eight passenger trains a day stopped there en route to Kansas City, Denver, or Chicago, and travelers got off to eat at a hotel near the station, a mile to the south along the Republican River. (The railroad dining car had not yet been invented.)

A horse-drawn streetcar traveled regularly along the main street, Webster, which ran north and south, and sometimes brought passengers into town from the train. Often they were executives of the Burlington Railroad who had come to visit Silas Garber and his wife; the Garbers lived in a spacious house on the eastern outskirts of Red Cloud. Everyone in town was familiar with the Garber house; local families often picnicked in the grove of cottonwood trees next to his property. Other landmarks in Red Cloud included the State Bank Building, a tall brick structure in the center of the business district, and J. L. Miner's General Store, a block to the south, where Willie had made her famous recitation when her father bought her new shoes. In the year following the Cathers' move into town another notable building, the Opera House, was erected a block to the north, over a hardware store and across the street from Dr. Cook's Drug Store.

Charles Cather opened his real estate and insurance office in a building next door to Miner's General Store. He settled his family a block away, in a rented house at the corner of Third and Cedar streets that would be their home for the next twenty years. The small frame cottage was attractive but cramped, and Willie and her brothers had to share a dormitory-style bedroom in the attic.

Willa Cather's attic bedroom in Red Cloud. Cather earned the wallpaper at Dr. Cook's Drug Store and hung it herself.

When Willie grew older, one wing of the attic was partitioned to make a separate space for her that became a study as well as a bedroom. As a teenager, she took a job at Dr. Cook's Drug Store, which carried a variety of items, and asked to be paid with wallpaper instead of money. She covered the walls of her room with the paper, a soft pattern of red and brown roses on a yellow background. More than a century later, the faded paper still lines the walls of Willa Cather's very first room of her own.

Willie entered the local elementary school soon after moving to Red Cloud. In her second year she was taught by Miss Evangeline King, the principal, who became an important influence in her life. Willie worked hard to please Miss King and later described her as "the first person whom I ever cared a great deal for outside of my own family."[1] Willie became closer to Miss King than to her own mother, and as she grew older turned to her for advice and encouragement.

Two other teachers became influential during Willie's high school years in Red Cloud: Mr. and Mrs. A. K. Goudy. Mrs. Goudy was the high school principal; her husband, the superintendent of schools, taught Latin. Willie, who valued long-term friendships throughout her life, wrote to Mrs. Goudy for more than forty years after leaving Red Cloud.

When Willie was not attending school she sometimes helped her mother care for her younger brothers and sisters. During the Cathers' first decade in Red Cloud, three more children were born—James, Elsie, and Jack. Willie didn't care much for housework, but she loved to play games with the children and read to them. She also organized "expeditions" to Far Island, a sandbar in the middle of the Republican River that was a special haunt of Red Cloud's children. In the wintertime ice skating and sledding were favorite pastimes.

Outside of her family, Willie's best younger friends in Red Cloud were J. L. Miner's four daughters, especially Carrie and Irene, whom she remained close to throughout her life. With the Miners and other neighborhood children, Willie put on short plays, or "theatricals," in her own home and in the Miners' parlor. In February 1888 Willie and the Miner daughters presented a benefit performance of *Beauty and the Beast* at the town's new Opera House. Willie, wearing a black wax mustache, appeared as the Merchant, Beauty's father. Proceeds from the performance were given to victims of a devastating blizzard.

The Opera House was a fascinating place for Willie and her friends. During the winter traveling companies of actors and singers visited for a week at a time to present plays and operettas to area residents. Posters announced their upcoming performances, and the excited children hung around the train station and the local hotel to see the performers. Everyone wanted to attend each show at least once; Willie and her friends often went twice, on opening and closing nights.

The shows, many of them musicals, probably encouraged Willie to develop the passion for music that increased as she grew older. The family had a piano, and Jennie Cather hired a teacher to give her oldest child lessons. Willie, however, never learned how to play; she was more interested in having her teacher, a German immigrant, play for *her*. She also encouraged him to relate stories of his musical experiences abroad.

What attracted Cather to music was its emotional power, its ability to express and evoke feeling. Julia Miner, the mother of her best friends, was another figure in her life who made music attractive. Mrs. Miner, who had emigrated from Norway, was the daughter of a musician with the Royal Norwegian Orchestra and as a child had been trained as a pianist. In her Red Cloud parlor she often played for her own pleasure, and the children would gather to listen. Willie was entranced by her music-making and also liked to hear stories about her life in Norway.

The Miner household held another attraction for Willie: the Bohemian hired girl Annie Sadilek, whose family lived on a farm on the Divide. Shortly after arriving in Nebraska, Willie had heard the story of Annie's father, Francis Sadilek. The story was not appropriate for a small child's ears, but the curious Willie had probably eavesdropped as she heard adults describing the Bohemian farmer's sad fate.

Sadilek had been a violinist in his native city of Prague before immigrating to America, but the harsh living conditions on the Divide as he struggled to provide for his wife and children finally overwhelmed him. One night, in despair, he had smashed his violin, then shot himself; he was buried at a crossroads east of town.

The story of Francis Sadilek haunted Willie. Often, back in her room, she and Carrie Miner discussed the tragedy and wondered together how Sadilek could have been driven to such a terrible act. Willie was captivated by his daughter Annie, who sent her wages to her family on the farm. She loved to watch the graceful, charming girl go about her work, and—as Willie did so often with other immigrants—she would coax Annie to tell stories of "life before," of the family's years in Prague.

Francis Sadilek in his lonely grave, his daughter Annie cheerfully working to support her family: Willie loved both of them as if they were her own family. Decades later their stories would become known to millions all over the world.

Books and reading continued to be important to Willie in Red Cloud. She still had her family's large library of classics to choose from, of course, and more recently published books were sold at the drugstore. These ranged from popular fiction to works by outstanding contemporary authors, including the Scot Robert Louis Stevenson, the American Mark Twain, and Russian novelist Leo Tolstoy. Stevenson's *Treasure Island*, published in 1883, was a special favorite, and Willie and her brothers liked to pretend they were pirates when they played on Far Island. In her early teens Willie "devoured" *Anna Karenina* and other books by Tolstoy.

Like her wallpaper, much of Willie's reading material was probably obtained in exchange for clerking at the drugstore. Another source was the library of Mr. and Mrs. Charles Wiener, a German-Jewish immigrant couple who owned a store in Red Cloud and lived around the corner from the Cathers. The Wieners owned a number of French and German classics in translation and happily loaned them to their bright neighbor.

Willie's other adult friends included an Englishman named William Ducker, who worked as a clerk in his brother's store. Shortly after his arrival in Red Cloud in 1885, the educated Ducker began giving Latin and Greek lessons to the eleven-year-old girl. During the next five years they read many of the ancient classics together, including works by Homer, Virgil, Ovid, and Anacreon. Ducker was also interested in science and let her perform experiments with him in his home laboratory.

Because of Ducker, Willie's interest in science grew. By the time she was a teenager she had decided to become a doctor. She had been inspired by the Cather family's own physician,

Dr. G. E. McKeeby, who had treated her for the mysterious paralytic disease she had suffered on the Divide. After the Cathers moved into Red Cloud, Willie liked to ride with the doctor in his horse-and-buggy as he made his rounds. (Until the mid-twentieth century, most American doctors treated patients in their own homes if they were too ill to come to their offices.)

Another inspiring doctor was a Red Cloud physician named Robert Damerell, and Willie often accompanied him on house calls, too. During one home visit she administered chloroform, an anesthetic, to a young boy while Dr. Damerell amputated the boy's leg. This incident, she later wrote, inspired her to become a surgeon. To prepare for her future career, she set up a small laboratory adjacent to her father's real estate office and dissected dogs and cats.

Willie had always been a tomboy, and her choice of what was then a virtually all-male profession was not especially surprising. For several years, however, ever since Willie had become a teenager, her mother and some of the townspeople had been disturbed by the girl's eccentric behavior. In an era when girls were supposed to look typically feminine, with long hair and frilly dresses, Willie cut her hair shorter than a man's, wore men's clothes and a derby, and carried a cane. Although several years earlier she had rewritten her birth name as "Willa" in the family Bible, the aspiring doctor now signed herself "William Cather, M.D." on school papers, and in theatricals she preferred male roles. This masculine disguise—her version of teenage rebellion—lasted until her second year in college.

Willie was busy throughout her high school years. She was an excellent student in the classroom. Away from school she continued her scientific experiments, staged plays with the Miner girls, and improved her Latin and Greek through further study with William Ducker. She also wrote a column about events at

*Webster Street, Red Cloud, Nebraska, during a political rally for William
Jennings Bryan in the summer of 1889. The tall building on the right is the
Farmers and Merchants Bank, built that year by Silas Garber. The building
on the left, behind the clock, is Dr. Cook's Drug Store, where Willa
worked as a teenager.*

the high school for an area newspaper, the *Webster County
Argus*. And there was always time for trips to the Divide to
visit Uncle George and his family, and to a ranch that the Miners owned outside of town.

On a warm June evening in 1890, Willa Cather,
age sixteen, and two young men—the entire senior class—
graduated from Red Cloud High School in a ceremony at the
Opera House. All three graduates made speeches. The men
spoke first, on topics related to self-advancement in business.
And then it was Willa's turn. Her ten-minute oration, entitled
"Superstition versus Investigation," was a defense of scientific
inquiry from antiquity to the present day. "All human history
is a record of an emigration," she began, "an exodus from bar-
barism to civilization."

It was a remarkable speech for someone so young to make,

and the audience was both pleased and astonished. The local newspaper, the *Red Cloud Chief*, reprinted all three speeches in its issue of June 13, 1890, and praised Willa's as "a masterpiece of oratory."[2] However, the newspaper article went on to predict great futures only for the two men; no mention was made of Willa's promise, perhaps because few people believed that her plans to become a doctor had any chance of succeeding.

Long before Willa Cather was a senior in high school, she was already thinking about attending college—specifically, the State University in Lincoln. The medical career that she planned required advanced training, but that did not mean receiving a university education. In the nineteenth century there were only a handful of medical schools in the United States, and they were located in large cities. Young men in rural areas who wanted to become doctors usually served an apprenticeship with local physicians, helping out with patients while they studied Gray's *Anatomy* and other medical textbooks from the doctor's library.

Willie was not a man, however, and the study of medicine was not encouraged among young women. It would have been very difficult for Willie or any other woman to find a doctor willing to take on a female apprentice. Willie would need formal medical training in a university if she was to achieve her goal.

In the late 1800s, only a relatively small number of people in the United States attended college—perhaps less than 70,000, three-fourths of them men, out of a total population of some 62 million in 1890. In fact, a grade school education was the norm; even completing high school at that time was considered a distinction, although female high school graduates outnumbered men. To everyone who knew her, however, it was clear that Willie deserved the chance for a college education no matter what she chose to study. Even her mother, who could never understand why Willie insisted on dressing like a boy, recognized that her daughter was gifted and needed further training.

There was only one problem: money.

By today's standards, a year at the university was hardly expensive. No money was charged for tuition; only a registration fee of $10.00 was required, plus a refundable deposit of another $10.00 to use the science laboratory. Books and other study materials cost a few more dollars. Room and meals in a Lincoln boardinghouse—there were no dormitories then at the university—were no more than $3.00 a week. Thus a student could get by easily during a nine-month school term on less than $150.

But by 1890 Charles Cather was still struggling to establish his business and to support his wife and children. The sum of $150 represented a major part of a year's income. Charles knew how much his oldest child wanted to go to college, however, and with his wife's encouragement he borrowed the money. In September 1890, accompanied by her mother, Willa Cather traveled by train to Lincoln, 150 miles away, to enroll at the State University.

THREE

University Days

When Willa Cather arrived in Lincoln in the fall of 1890, she still planned to become a doctor. However, there had already been several indications that she would have a career in writing, not medicine. One was her eloquent graduation address. Another had occurred when she was not quite fifteen.

In the nineteenth and early twentieth centuries, young women often passed around albums in which their friends recorded "Opinions, Tastes and Fancies." On October 10, 1888, Willa wrote in a girlfriend's album that her favorite color was "sea green," that her favorite composer was Beethoven, and that her "chief ambition in life" was "to be an M.D." But to the question of "who had rendered the greatest service towards the world's progress," Willa answered "Cadmus."[1]

Cadmus, however, was not a scientist or a physician. He was a Phoenician prince who had introduced writing to the ancient Greeks.

Before Willa could formally enroll in the University of Nebraska, she had to spend a year in the preparatory division, a two-year program offering additional training in classical languages, literature, and the sciences. The university, founded in 1869, had a strong academic reputation and had attracted leading scholars to its faculty. Red Cloud High School had not prepared Willa to meet the university's high entrance requirements.

All during her preparatory year Willa maintained her male persona: she wore her hair short, dressed in men's starched shirts, spoke in a deep voice, and signed her name "William." There was one concession to femininity: she wore skirts, not trousers, though they were not as long as fashion—or respectability—required.

Willa studied intensely and did well in her courses. Her personality seemed very different from the rest of her family, who were relaxed and gentle; Willa was energetic and often brusque. Classmates later recalled that she was either loved or hated; no one seemed to be indifferent to her. Willa had her own circle of friends, including another student named Louise Pound and Louise's brother Roscoe, who taught botany. Roscoe, who was also a lawyer, later became a prominent jurist and dean of the Harvard Law School; Louise became a well-known folklore scholar and served as the first woman president of the Modern Language Association.

For relaxation Willa appeared in campus plays, usually taking male roles as she had done in Red Cloud. She also enjoyed attending Lincoln's two theaters, the Lansing and the Funke, which together seated 3,000. The city of Lincoln, founded at about the same time as the university, had become a thriving railroad center by 1890 with a population of 35,000. Its residents eagerly looked forward to seeing world-famous actors and musicians on their tours of major cities. Trains brought as many as one hundred different orchestras, opera companies, and theater troupes to Lincoln each year. Willa found it thrilling to sit in the cavernous, ornately decorated theaters to hear electrifying musical and dramatic performances.

In her preparatory year at the university, Willa took several courses in literature. In February 1891 one of her literature professors assigned his class a theme on the topic "The Personal Characteristics of Thomas Carlyle." Willa was excited by the subject; she had already read several works by Carlyle, a prominent Scottish historian and essayist who had died ten years earlier.

Willa's theme on Carlyle astonished her professor, who thought it was so outstanding that he submitted it to the *Nebraska State Journal*, a newspaper published in Lincoln. Willa's essay appeared in the paper on the following Sunday, together with an editorial praising her for her talent. Its publication marked the official beginning of her writing career.

The Carlyle essay was also significant because it set forth Willa's own beliefs about art and literature and the craft of writing. The artist, she wrote, had to be dedicated totally to his art: "Art of every kind is an exacting master,"[2] she said. She emphasized that self-discipline and hard work were central to the life of any true artist.

Many years later Willa recalled how proud she had been to see her name and her writing in print, although she did not immediately abandon her desire to become a doctor. During the summer of 1891, back home in Red Cloud, she continued her scientific investigations, including the dissection of frogs to study their circulatory system.

In September, however, when Willa was admitted officially to the university as a first-year student, she did not enroll in any science courses; instead she studied Greek and Latin, as well as English composition, and was allowed to take a junior-level class on the plays of William Shakespeare. She also took freshman mathematics, which was very difficult for her; only in the second semester of her senior year did Willa finally manage to pass the math course, a requirement for graduation.

Early in the fall of her freshman year, Willa wrote an essay entitled "Shakespeare and *Hamlet*" for her Shakespeare class. It, too, impressed her professor and was published in two parts in the *Journal*. Willa's interest in writing blossomed. She became

Cather about 1894, working at the Nebraska State Journal *in Lincoln. Her earnings as a journalist paid for much of her college education.*

an associate editor, with her friend Louise Pound, of a campus magazine called *Lasso* and also joined the university's Union Literary Society.

In her freshman year Willa accomplished another milestone: she published her first short story, a tale that she titled "Peter." She had submitted the story to her composition instructor, who sent it along to a Boston magazine called *The Mahogany Tree.* "Peter" appeared in its May 1892 issue. "Peter" was the thinly disguised story of Francis Sadilek, the Bohemian farmer who had shot himself on the Divide years earlier. Willa's first published story expressed what became a lifelong fascination with artists and their frustrated lives. She later published several revised versions of the tale and also used it in her novel *My Ántonia.*

In her three remaining years at the university, Willa's extracurricular activities were mostly literary. As a sophomore she became associate editor of *Hesperian*, the campus literary journal. She began contributing short stories and plays to *Hesperian*—including a revised version of "Peter"—and the following year she was named the magazine's managing editor; she also served as the literary editor of the yearbook. She continued her interest in drama as well, appearing in campus plays in both male and female roles.

In her junior year Willa made her debut as a paid writer when she was invited by the *Nebraska State Journal* to contribute a weekly column to the newspaper entitled "One Way of Putting It." The column, which was unsigned, appeared for the first time on Sunday, November 5, 1893. Willa was pleased, of course, to have a regular outlet for her literary talent—she could include almost anything she cared to write about in the columns, both fact and fiction.

Willa was also happy to have a regular source of income because her father had been having financial difficulties back in Red Cloud and money was scarce. At first she was paid a dollar per column; later she was assigned articles that appeared under her byline and earned her more money. During her junior year Willa received $65.00 from the newspaper, enough to cover a substantial part of her room and board.

With responsibility for course work—she studied history and philosophy as well as languages and literature—her newspaper job, and her extracurricular literary and dramatic activities, Willa was very busy at the university. She was also moving closer to a career as a professional writer. Although she was an excellent student—in every subject but mathematics—she knew that she did not want a career as a scholar. In fact, she often criticized some of her professors for taking the joy out of great works of literature by overanalyzing them.

As her knowledge increased, her tastes became more

refined and specialized. Back in Red Cloud she had first become interested in French literature through books loaned to her by Mr. and Mrs. Wiener. In Lincoln that interest grew until it became a consuming passion. She learned to read the French language well and became an enthusiastic admirer of all forms of French culture. In particular, she liked the works of the great nineteenth-century novelist Gustave Flaubert, especially his most famous book, *Madame Bovary*.

By the middle of her junior year, Willa's assignments for the *Journal* included theater criticism. As a reviewer she received free tickets to attend plays, an opportunity that she relished. Her drama reviews were frank, fearless, and often negative, and readers were entertained by her lively writing style.

After several months, in the spring of 1894, she became the *Journal*'s regular drama critic as her reputation spread throughout the Midwest and beyond. Actors and their managers were put on notice to perform well—or receive a scathing review from "that meatax young girl," as the *Journal*'s managing editor, Will Owen Jones, later described her.[3] During the summer—when the theater season ended—Willa sent articles to the *Journal* from Red Cloud on various topics, including her first long feature story, an account of an abandoned pioneer town, Brownville, that had been the first settlement in Nebraska Territory.

In her senior year Willa had to drop many of her extracurricular activities because of increased newspaper work, which she needed to earn money. In nine months she contributed ninety-five pieces—drama reviews, columns, and feature stories—to the *Journal* while attending college full-time. As a journalist-critic she met well-known figures who passed through Lincoln, including Stephen Crane, the author of *The Red Badge of Courage*. She also attended many gatherings at the home of a famous local resident, the politician William Jennings Bryan, who later became a U.S. presidential candidate.

Cather poses in her college graduation ball gown, June 1895.

In March 1895, several months before graduation, Willa ful-
filled a long-held dream: she traveled to Chicago to hear a
series of operas presented by stars of the Metropolitan Opera
Company of New York City. For an entire week Willa was in
ecstasy as she attended nightly performances of works by
Verdi, Meyerbeer, and Gounod. She wrote a glowing review of
one of the operas, Verdi's *Falstaff*, for the *Journal*. (There may
have been at least one explanation of her special fondness for

this opera: *Falstaff* was based on a character who appears in several plays by Shakespeare. Willa knew Shakespeare's works thoroughly and admired him as one of her favorite authors.)

When she returned to Lincoln, Willa came down with a flulike ailment that was diagnosed as "typhoid-pneumonia." Normally healthy, she now had to spend several weeks in bed, probably as a consequence of overwork and fatigue. This was the first time she had suffered from a serious illness since her childhood bout with what may have been polio. Nevertheless, she finished her class work and also wrote nearly two dozen more newspaper articles during April, May, and early June.

Finally, on June 12, 1895, graduation day arrived and Willa received her bachelor of arts degree. During her years in Lincoln, Willa had gradually abandoned her masculine persona, allowed her chestnut brown hair to grow, and replaced starched shirts with dresses that flattered her medium height and build. For the university's graduation ball she wore an elegant gown of ivory net and satin, trimmed with gold sequins. Her school days were over.

Willa Cather was now a college graduate, but she lacked a full-time job. She continued to write articles and reviews for the *Journal* and was also hired as a part-time staff writer for a local weekly called the *Courier*. She still made her home in Lincoln but stayed in Red Cloud for part of the summer. By Christmastime finances forced her to leave the boardinghouse in Lincoln for good and live at home.

Although she felt discouraged, Willa continued to enhance her reputation through her newspaper articles. In January 1896 she was invited to address a convention of the Nebraska Newspaper Association, and after the meeting other journalists from around the state—nearly all men—praised her competence and predicted a great future for her.

Between assignments she helped her mother care for the three youngest children, Jim, Elsie, and Jack. She wrote to friends back in Lincoln that she was also trying her hand at writing short stories again, an occupation she had not had time for during the months when she was trying to go to school and earn her living simultaneously. She placed two short stories—accounts of immigrant life on the Divide—in Nebraska literary journals.

During this period Willa Cather had the opportunity to read even more than before, and in her newspaper articles she wrote less about theatrical events and increasingly about literature. She reviewed current fiction by leading novelists of the day, including William Dean Howells and Henry James; she was not fond of Howells but admired James extravagantly as a "mighty master of language and keen student of human actions and motives."[4] She also wrote articles that praised literary masters of the recent past, including the American writer Nathaniel Hawthorne and a childhood favorite, Robert Louis Stevenson. The English critic John Ruskin was also a favorite writer of Willa Cather's. When the French poet Paul Verlaine died during the winter of 1896, she lauded him—and all the literature of France—in a long column in the *Journal*.

Still she was restless and longed for a full-time job. She tried to get a teaching appointment at the university and was deeply disappointed when she was not hired. By springtime she was feeling very discouraged—and then, in May, the tide turned. The publishers of a women's magazine, *Home Monthly*, based in Pittsburgh, Pennsylvania, offered her a job as an assistant editor. She eagerly accepted.

Precisely how *Home Monthly* and Willa Cather were brought together is not known. Most Cather biographers have assumed that the offer resulted from known ties between staff members of the *Nebraska Journal* and the *Home Monthly* publishers. Regardless of how it came about, the job began a dramatic new chapter in Willa Cather's life. In late June of 1896 she moved to Pittsburgh. It would be her home for ten years.

FOUR

Apprenticeship in Pittsburgh

W illa Cather had become fond of the Nebraska
prairie during her growing-up years, but she was
still nostalgic for her Virginia birthplace. Riding
the train to Pittsburgh, her first trip beyond Chicago since
moving to the Divide, Cather was delighted to see the flat bare
landscape transform itself into rolling hills, studded with
masses of green trees and patches of blue water. Western
Pennsylvania did not look all that different from Back Creek
Valley, less than 150 miles from Pittsburgh.

Upon her arrival, Cather lived for several weeks with her
new boss, James Axtell, the publisher of *Home Monthly*, and his
family, but she found Axtell's wife and daughters prim and
priggish. By mid-July she had saved enough money to move to
a boardinghouse not far from her office, on the east side of
Pittsburgh. Cather had been hired as an assistant editor of the
Home Monthly at a salary of $100.00 a month, but she was soon
doing most of the work on the magazine herself, everything
from writing articles to preparing layouts at the printshop.

At first she did not find the work very rewarding: the magazine focused on housekeeping and child care, two subjects
that did not interest Cather in the least. Under her editorship,
however, the *Home Monthly* became a more lively journal that

Union Station, Pittsburgh, in the 1890s. Cather arrived here from Nebraska in June 1896 to edit the Home Monthly. *On the hill at right is Central High School, where she would later teach.*

included articles on a variety of interesting topics. Cather had to include pieces—written by other contributors—on traditional women's interests like cooking and sewing, but she herself wrote feature stories on the wives of U.S. presidential candidates William Jennings Bryan and William McKinley, Queen Victoria's Diamond Jubilee, and well-known contemporary writers. She also contributed a monthly book column to the magazine. Cather was trying to expand the intellects of her female readers beyond house cleaning, meal planning, and laundry—and she was also making her job more interesting. Happily no one discouraged her.

In addition, Cather published nine of her own short stories in the magazine; Axtell, always encouraging, allowed her time off occasionally to write fiction. Years later, after she had become famous, Cather dismissed these early stories as unimportant and blocked attempts to republish them. Two were fairy tales that she had made up for her youngest brothers and sister back in Nebraska; the others were serious narratives of contemporary life.

Although Cather's short stories from this period are amateurish, they are interesting for several reasons. For one thing, Cather avoided at least one pitfall of the budding fiction writer: she did not write about exotic subjects in foreign locales. Instead, she used settings with which she had some familiarity—Nebraska, Chicago, Pittsburgh—and created recognizable characters, including a tomboy like herself who moves East but misses her Nebraska home ("Tommy, the Unsentimental"), a disillusioned opera singer ("Nanette: An Aside"), and a ne'er-do-well son who is finally reconciled with his parents ("The Burglar's Christmas").

Cather's *Home Monthly* stories are also interesting because they foreshadow elements in her later work. First, music and musicians, which became increasingly important in Cather's life and art, play a prominent role in several of the stories. Second, nearly all of them are told from a male point of view, a device she would adopt in most of her later fiction. Finally, in these stories Cather quietly introduces a theme that runs throughout her work: a negative view of marriage.

In more ways than one, Cather was challenging the assumptions of the half million women in western Pennsylvania who were *Home Monthly*'s readers.

Despite the demands of her full-time job, the resourceful Cather was determined to continue her career as a critic. Within a few months of her arrival in Pittsburgh, she had secured a part-time position as music and drama critic for one of the city's newspapers, the *Pittsburgh Leader*. She rewrote many of these articles and sent them back to the *Nebraska Journal*, which published them under the title of her old column, "The Passing Show."

Attending plays, concerts, and operas was hardly work for

Cather, and writing about performances was a pleasure that also earned her a salary. In fact, the city's cultural events were at the center of an abundant social life that Cather enjoyed during the decade she spent in Pittsburgh.

With a population of 400,000 at the turn of the century, Pittsburgh was a thriving metropolis whose wealth came from steel mills and other types of manufacturing. Its leading industrialists included Andrew Carnegie, Andrew Mellon, George Westinghouse, and Henry Clay Frick, all of whom were patrons of the arts. Carnegie had donated money to build a library, an art gallery, and a concert hall.

Cather often visited the Carnegie Library, which was located near her office, and also spent many hours at the Carnegie Art Gallery. She was pleased most of all by the number of concerts offered at Pittsburgh's Carnegie Hall; as a bona fide newspaper critic, she could attend them at little or no charge.

Cather had a number of friends, both male and female, in Pittsburgh. Immediately after her arrival, the Axtells had begun introducing her to the city's cultural elite, but she preferred making friends on her own. Some of them were writers like herself whom she had met through the local press club or because they had submitted articles to the magazine, like George Seibel and his wife, Helen. As a regular patron of the library, she met and began a lifelong friendship with the director, Edwin Anderson, and his wife; Anderson later became head of the New York Public Library after Cather moved to New York City.

· Another lifelong friend was Dorothy Canfield, whom Cather had met in Lincoln when Canfield's father had taught at the university. Cather and Canfield, who was six years younger, shared an intense interest in literature. Canfield herself later became a well-known novelist, writing under her married name, Dorothy Canfield Fisher. After Cather's move to Pittsburgh, Dorothy Canfield's father had become president of Ohio State University, and Canfield enrolled as a student there. She often visited Cather in Pittsburgh before settling in

Vermont in 1907 following her marriage.

Cather missed her large family, and the household of George and Helen Seibel, who were about the same age as she was, provided domestic comfort. Cather spent many evenings with the couple, enjoying conversations about literature and reading French and German classics with them. Sometimes they baked cookies together, and at Christmastime Cather helped trim their tree. When the Seibels had a baby, she enjoyed playing with the little girl and buying presents for her.

Cather had a fun-loving side, too: traveling to and from work on a bicycle, she mischievously raced trolley cars through the streets of Pittsburgh. A victory always cheered her.

After more than a year at the *Home Monthly*, Cather was offered a full-time job as telegraph editor of the *Pittsburgh Leader* at a salary of $75.00 a month. This was less than her former salary, but the newspaper was a far more prestigious publication than the *Home Monthly*. Cather made extra money by writing special features for the *Leader* as well as continuing her drama and music reviews, sometimes using different pseudonyms. Her Nebraska columns also continued, although she now sent them to the *Lincoln Courier* instead of the *Journal*.

As the telegraph editor on a leading newspaper, Cather had a demanding job—and one usually reserved for men—but she approached it with her usual energy. From 8:00 in the morning until 2:00 each afternoon she received cables from correspondents in foreign countries that reported brief news items. Cather had to expand these cables into substantial news stories, which often required her to do research in history and current affairs. After work ended in the afternoon she had time to do her own writing, and then to attend concerts and plays in the evening.

During her first year at the *Leader*, Cather made another friend, a well-known composer named Ethelbert Nevin. Nevin, then thirty-five, was a member of a socially prominent Pittsburgh family. He had recently returned to the city after living abroad for a decade. Throughout her life Cather worshiped men and women whom she considered true artists and had intensely emotional relationships with several of them. Nevin was the first "genuine artist" she had ever known personally, and Cather enjoyed many hours in his company. She was obviously starstruck, and the flattered Nevin responded by accompanying her to concerts, talking at length with her at parties at which the two were guests, and giving her small presents.

Nevin, however, was married and had two children, and some of their mutual friends questioned the wisdom of Cather's behavior. However, Cather had had unconventional relationships before with older men, including a middle-aged doctor in Lincoln who had been her escort for several years. She was not about to bow to gossip over what was, after all, an innocent friendship. She wrote a profile of the composer that was published in the *Ladies' Home Journal* in 1900 and included photographs she had taken of him. Gradually, Nevin withdrew from the relationship under pressure from his wife, but Cather mourned him intensely when he died suddenly in 1901. Two dozen years later she would immortalize him in a memorable short story, "Uncle Valentine."

Cather did not have traditional feminine interests, nor did she feel comfortable in frills, bustles, and other ornamentation. Her clothing, like her personality, was crisp and tailored. Nevertheless, she had a number of male suitors, several of whom proposed marriage. One was Charles Moore, the nephew of her father's boss, with whom she was close friends during her years in Lincoln. The relationship had ended by the time she moved to Pittsburgh, but for the rest of her life she wore a gift he had given her: a gold ring in the shape of a serpent. Another marriage proposal came from Preston Farrar, who taught English at Allegheny High School in Pittsburgh. Cather also declined Farrar's offer, although she continued her friendship with him and the woman he later married.

The most important friendship of Willa Cather's life was her close relationship with Isabelle McClung, a member of a socially prominent Pittsburgh family. McClung, who was four years younger than Cather, was the daughter of a judge. The two first met in the winter of 1899 in the dressing room of an actress whom they had just seen perform in a play. Cather was there to interview the actress, Lizzie Hudson Collier; McClung, who had a passionate interest in art and drama, had gone backstage to meet Collier.

The two young women immediately liked each other; for Cather, McClung became the person she most deeply cherished for the rest of her life. Two years after their meeting, Cather moved into the McClung house on Murray Hill Avenue, in a fashionable neighborhood called Squirrel Hill, and lived there until she left the city in 1906. A small sewing room on the third floor was converted into a study for Cather. There, encouraged by McClung, Cather began to write the first stories that she considered "serious art" and worthy of preserving.

Although Cather was devoted to another woman for most of her life, and although she decided to forgo permanent romantic attachments to the opposite sex, she did not dislike men. In fact, male relationships were always important to her from childhood onward, and some of her closest friends were male.

Cather believed, however, that no serious artist, male or female, could be happily married; all forms of art required single-minded attention. "In the kingdom of art there is no God but one . . . and his service is so exacting that there are few men born of woman who are strong enough to take the vows,"[1] she had written shortly before leaving Nebraska. By the time she reached her mid-twenties, Cather had decided to be married only to her writing.

FIVE

Breaking New Ground

L ater in life, after Willa Cather had become famous, she often spoke with fondness of her apprenticeship in Pittsburgh, years during which she was honing her skills as a writer. At the time she was living there, however, many of her friends and colleagues thought she had already reached the apex of her career: she had, after all, distinguished herself in the traditionally male field of journalism.

But Cather was not satisfied with herself. She knew that she was working toward something greater than routine newspaper work. She continued to write fiction whenever she had the opportunity, and in the fall of 1899 she had the satisfaction of selling her first short story to a national magazine, *Cosmopolitan* (a different publication from the late-twentieth-century magazine with the same name). Entitled "Eric Hermannson's Soul," the story was published in the April 1900 issue. The title character is a Nebraska farm boy, a Swedish immigrant who loves to play his fiddle and learns to enjoy life freely by escaping the restraints of a fundamentalist religious sect.

Many critics believe that "Eric Hermannson's Soul" represents a significant advance in Cather's ability to write fiction. For the first time she was able to make readers understand the story by her careful choice of details, especially her depiction of life on the Divide. As one critic, James Woodress, has written, she was *evoking*, or bringing forth a story from the material, not just *telling* it.

That same month another milestone occurred in Cather's life: she published her last article in the *Leader* and ended her full-time association with a daily newspaper. Shortly afterward she joined the staff of a weekly, the *Library*, and during the next six months published sixteen articles, seven poems, and five short stories—none of them important—in its pages. This employment earned her a living, but it was only temporary as Cather tried to decide how best to pursue a life in art.

A journalist friend from Nebraska now working in Chicago tried to persuade Cather to move to that city, but she decided against it. During her first three summers in the East she had returned to Red Cloud for vacations with her family, but in the summer of 1900 she remained in Pittsburgh, probably because she needed the salary from her job with the *Library*.

From her earliest days in Pittsburgh, Cather had been sending money home, a pattern that continued throughout her life. Cather was devoted to her family, and she felt especially obligated to help them because they had sacrificed to send her to college. She gave money not only to her parents but also to several of her siblings, beginning with her brother Roscoe when he was seriously ill during the winter of 1898 and unable to work. Roscoe, four years her junior and closest to her in both age and temperament, had not been able to afford college and had become a teacher after graduating from high school. (In the nineteenth century and well into the twentieth, many states did not require elementary and high school teachers to have college or university training.)

When the *Library* ceased publication in the fall of 1900, Cather considered returning to Nebraska to care for her mother, who was ill, and even asked her old boss at the *Journal* for a job. Instead she moved to Washington, D.C., where she lived with a cousin, Howard Gore, and got a temporary job translating letters and documents in French for a U.S. government commission. At the same time, the *Nebraska Journal* hired her as its

Washington correspondent; she also became a correspondent for the *Index of Pittsburgh Life,* the successor to the *Library.*

No one knows exactly why Cather left Pittsburgh at this time, although she had enjoyed the capital city during a visit there in 1898. Gore may have told her about the government job and she, in turn, may have welcomed the chance to spend time in Washington. Furthermore, she may have believed that she would have more opportunities to write fiction.

During the four months that Cather worked in Washington, from December 1900 until March 1901, she contributed more than two dozen reviews and columns to the *Journal* and *Index.* She also managed to write several short stories for widely read magazines. One of them, "Jack-a-Boy," was a tale about a youngster who resembled her youngest brother, Jack; it was published in the *Saturday Evening Post* in March 1901 and again gave her national exposure.

About this time Cather made another change in her name: she began calling herself Willa Sibert Cather, adapting a name from her mother's side of the family. (Grandmother Boak's maiden name was Seibert.) For two decades all her writing appeared under all three names, and occasionally she signed her newspaper reviews with the single name *Sibert.* Beginning in 1920 she dropped the middle name from the title pages of her books but continued to use it in other contexts. She always included the letter *S* in her monogram and used all three names in her will.

In March 1901 Cather returned abruptly to Pittsburgh to assume a new job. A vacancy had occurred at Central High School when a teacher resigned because of illness. Cather had probably learned of the opening from the McClungs, and her application was promptly accepted. For four months she taught Latin, English composition, and algebra. It was tiring work: she was exhausted by the time summer vacation arrived and had lost twenty pounds.

Back in Red Cloud for several months, Cather wrote articles and reviews for the *Lincoln Courier* on a variety of topics,
ranging from art and music to the condition of steelworkers in
Pennsylvania. In September she returned to Central as a full-
time English teacher. For Cather, who was never good at math,
no longer having to teach algebra must have been an enormous relief.

Cather taught English for two years at Central High School,
then succeeded her old suitor Preston Farrar as an English
teacher at Allegheny High School, across the river, for three
more years. Teaching was demanding, but Cather enjoyed it
and even believed for a while that she had found her true calling. At first her salary was relatively small—$650 for ten
months of work—but she had moved in with the McClungs
after returning from Washington and received free room and
board. She also continued to earn money as a free-lance journalist, contributing columns and reviews to the *Pittsburgh
Gazette*. By 1906, in her last year as a teacher, she was earning
the then-impressive annual salary of $1,300.

Cather hoped that school vacations throughout the year
would give her more time to write short stories; in 1901 she
announced to friends that she intended to write a novel, too.
For several years, however, she produced very little fiction. Her
disappointment at her lack of progress was offset somewhat
by her first trip abroad, which she made in the summer of
1902 with Isabelle McClung.

The two women toured England and France for three
months; Cather supplemented money she had saved for the
trip by selling a series of travel letters to the *Journal* back in
Nebraska. She was ecstatic at being able to immerse herself in
the culture of British and French writers whom she so much
admired, and she and McClung made leisurely explorations of
both countries. Undoubtedly there were two great moments
for Cather that summer: her meeting in London with the well-

known poet A. E. Housman, who had written *A Shropshire Lad*, and her sojourn in and around Rouen, France, the home of her beloved Gustave Flaubert.

Although Cather never thought of herself as a poet, she loved poetry and had been writing verse since childhood. In college she published poems in the campus literary magazine, and during her years in Pittsburgh she contributed poetry to the *Home Monthly*, the *Lincoln Courier*, the *Library*, and to national magazines, including *Harper's Weekly* and *Lippincott's*.

In 1903, eager to be known as the author of a book-length work, Cather allowed her poetry to be collected and printed by a Boston "vanity" publisher named Richard Badger. (Vanity publishers charge authors all or most of the costs of printing their books.) The collection was called *April Twilights* and included thirty-seven poems. Following the popular fashion of the time, nearly all of them were verses on themes from classical Greek and Roman literature.

April Twilights was reviewed favorably in a number of publications, including the *New York Times* and other major newspapers. Critics said that she showed promise. Cather was not interested in pursuing a career as a poet, however. During the more than four decades of her life that followed, she published only sixteen more poems and no new book-length collections. After Cather had become a well-known novelist, she authorized the publication in 1923 of a new edition of *April Twilights*, which omitted thirteen of the original poems and added twelve new ones. A new printing of the 1923 edition, to which she added another new poem, appeared in 1933.

By today's critical standards, none of the versions of *April Twilights* are memorable, but the book's first publication in 1903 is significant for two reasons. First, it gained Cather additional publicity as a writer who had been published by a well-known company (despite Badger's status as a vanity publisher). Second, it introduces themes and incidents she

*Wearing her everyday teaching outfit—shirtwaist, tie, and long skirt—
Cather posed for this portrait in 1903, possibly to commemorate the
publication of her first book,* April Twilights.

employed in her later fiction. Many of the poems express a
strong nostalgia for a past far more glorious than the present.

One poem, "Prairie Dawn," foreshadows one of Cather's
memorable strengths as a novelist as she writes with feeling
about the Nebraska landscape:

> *A crimson fire that vanquishes the stars;*
> *A pungent odor from the dusty sage;*
> *A sudden stirring of the huddled herds;*
> *A breaking of the distant table-lands*
> *Through purple mists ascending, and the flare*
> *Of water-ditches silver in the light;*
> *A swift, bright lance hurled low across the world;*
> *A sudden sickness for the hills of home.*[1]

"Prairie Dawn" is considered by most critics to be the best poem in the collection—and therefore the best poem that Cather ever wrote.

About the time that *April Twilights* was first published, a famous New York editor named S. S. McClure was becoming interested in Willa Cather's short stories. McClure was the publisher of *McClure's Magazine,* a popular monthly that included fiction as well as articles on topics of current interest. A few months earlier, McClure had launched what became known as the "muckraking movement" in the United States, publishing a series of investigative articles on corruption in American business, municipal government, and labor unions.

McClure sent scouts throughout the country to search for new writing talent, and one of them met Will Owen Jones, Cather's former boss at the *Nebraska State Journal.* Jones recommended Cather's work, and in late April 1903 McClure sent her a letter, inviting her to submit stories for possible publication. Cather was doubtful—her work had been rejected by *McClure's* in the past—but she dutifully mailed several of them to McClure. A week later she received a telegram from the publisher, asking her to come to New York City immediately to meet with him.

As soon as she could arrange for a substitute teacher, Cather went to New York, and on the morning of May 1, 1903, she presented herself at his office. McClure's first words to her were astonishing: henceforth, he wanted to publish *all* her stories in his magazine and later in book form. (He claimed he had never seen the stories she had submitted earlier; an assistant editor had returned them to her.) Here was the break Cather had never dreamed possible: a publisher was actively pursuing her and might single-handedly launch her career.

McClure's enthusiasm for her work did not mean that Cather could now devote herself full-time to writing. She still considered schoolteaching her primary occupation and taught for three more years, writing fiction only when she could find a spare moment.

Nor did McClure keep his promise and publish every story she sent him during this period. He ran only two in *McClure's Magazine*—"The Sculptor's Funeral" and "Paul's Case"—and not until 1905, the same year he published her book as he had promised. Both of those stories were included in the book, which Cather named *The Troll Garden*. (The title comes from a passage in *The Roman and the Teuton*, by the nineteenth-century English writer Charles Kingsley, in which he describes "a fairy garden" of trolls "working at their magic forges, making and making always things rare and strange.")[2]

There are five other stories in *The Troll Garden*: "'A Death in the Desert'" (the only other story in the collection that had been published elsewhere, in *Scribner's Magazine*), "Flavia and Her Artists," "A Wagner Matinee," "The Marriage of Phaedra," and "The Garden Lodge." All seven stories concern the problems that creative, artistic people face in a world that is indifferent and often destructive to their sensitivity and talents.

"Paul's Case" is the best-known of the seven and may be the most famous story that Cather ever wrote; it has been widely anthologized and was dramatized on public television. Although the main character, Paul, is not an artist, he has what Cather would call an artistic temperament. As a Pittsburgh high school student who loves the theater and is bored with his courses, Paul dreams of a more exciting life. When he neglects his schoolwork, his father and the principal decide he should leave school and get a job.

Paul rebels, steals money from his employer, and catches a train to New York, where he rents an expensive suite at the elegant Waldorf-Astoria Hotel and masquerades for a while as a wealthy patron of the arts. Finally, with his money used up and his father about to take him back to Pittsburgh, Paul jumps in front of a train.

He felt something strike his chest, and that his body was being thrown swiftly through the air, on and on, immeasurably far and fast, while his limbs were gently relaxed. Then, because the picture making mechanism was crushed, the disturbing visions flashed into black, and Paul dropped back into the immense design of things.[3]

Cather was proud of *The Troll Garden* and delighted to see a book of her stories in print, but reviewers were not enthusiastic. A few thought that Cather showed promise, but most of them criticized her for being too sympathetic to "freaks," people at odds with their environment. They saw nothing appealing in characters like Paul, or the once musically gifted Aunt Georgiana in "A Wagner Matinee" who has been turned into a wretched hag by the harsh life of the Nebraska prairie.

Cather was not discouraged. In the summer of 1905 she and Isabelle McClung—to whom *The Troll Garden* was dedicated—traveled west, stopping first in Red Cloud for several weeks. The two women spent the remainder of the summer camping out in Wyoming and South Dakota.

In September Cather was back again at Allegheny High School for what she assumed would be another full year of teaching. McClure had not forgotten her, however. In December, at his invitation, she returned East briefly to attend a seventieth-birthday party for Mark Twain, held in great splendor at Delmonico's restaurant in New York City.

Three months later, in March 1906, McClure came to Pittsburgh to see Cather with an urgent request: would she please take a temporary leave of absence from teaching and come to New York to help him edit his magazine? Excited by the offer, she left her classes in the hands of a substitute teacher, believing she would be back by the end of the summer.

By June Cather had changed her mind about the duration of her stay. In a farewell letter to her students, she wrote that "sudden and unforeseen" changes had caused her to resign from the faculty of Allegheny High School.[4] McClure had persuaded her to remain in New York City as one of his editors.

SIX

Making It in New York

Willa Cather's decision to settle in New York was not made as hastily as her abrupt departure from Pittsburgh would suggest. She had often dreamed of one day moving there, and there were logical reasons for her to make the city her permanent home. By the early twentieth century, New York had long held the title as the nation's most populous city and had displaced Boston as the cultural capital of the United States. As a center for literature, painting, and music, it was a natural place for aspiring artists to settle. Cather believed that recognition there as a literary artist was the highest honor to which she could aspire.

During her years in Pittsburgh, Cather had visited New York more than half a dozen times. Nearly everything important to her could be found there: opera, concerts, plays, and book and magazine publishers, as well as the opportunity for friendships with leading artists, musicians, and writers. Cather would always remember her Nebraska years, and the family and friends there who had nurtured her. Those years had given her material for her literary art. Now, in her new environment, Cather believed she would be encouraged to emerge as an artist in her own right. Before that could happen, however, she had to continue earning her living as a journalist.

Cather's work for *McClure's* was interesting, at least, even though it gave her little time to write fiction. She had the satisfaction of knowing that she was working for what many critics considered the best magazine in America at that time. In addition to its investigative articles, *McClure's* published short stories and serialized novels by some of the most famous writers in the Western world, including Rudyard Kipling, Joseph Conrad, Thomas Hardy, Robert Louis Stevenson, Stephen Crane, O. Henry, Jack London, and Mark Twain. In his magazine S. S. McClure also published interviews with famous men and women, and ran lengthy accounts of new scientific discoveries and inventions.

The magazine offices were located on East 23rd Street, in what was then the heart of the city's publishing district. During her first months in New York, Cather lived farther south in Manhattan, in a hotel on West 9th Street in the district called Greenwich Village. She could walk to work or ride one of the trolley cars that traveled up and down Fifth Avenue.

Many artists and writers lived in Greenwich Village, and Cather chose a more permanent home in the same area in the fall of 1906, when she moved into a studio apartment at 60 Washington Square South. A proofreader at *McClure's* named Edith Lewis lived in the same building. Cather had met Lewis three years earlier, during a trip home to Nebraska. Lewis, born and raised in Lincoln, had just graduated from Smith College in Massachusetts. The two women became friends, and Cather helped Lewis get her job at *McClure's*.

In 1908 Cather and Lewis moved together from Washington Square to a nearby apartment at 82 Washington Place. Lewis, a decade younger than Cather, became Cather's companion and personal assistant while she pursued her own career in advertising. The two women shared homes for the next thirty-nine years, until Cather's death in 1947.

Cather's duties as an editor at *McClure's* included buying fiction and poetry for the magazine and then editing these contributions. She also had to rewrite many of the nonfiction articles
that had been accepted by S. S. McClure, correcting grammar,
spelling, and sentence structure. When Cather proved her competence at these tasks, McClure assigned her to write a biography of Mary Baker Eddy, who had founded the Christian Science Church in Boston in 1879.

Writing the biography of Mrs. Eddy was hard work for
Cather, but its publication in installments during 1907 and
early 1908 brought *McClure's* lots of favorable publicity. (It was
not, however, published under Cather's name, at her request.
For some unknown reason, Cather always denied that she had
written the biography—perhaps because she did not want to
be associated with a nonliterary subject.) The magazine's circulation soared, and McClure rewarded Cather with a promotion to managing editor. He also allowed her time off for a second trip to Europe, and from April until August 1908 Cather
toured Italy with Isabelle McClung.

Writing the Eddy biography had an additional benefit for
Cather: her research took her to Boston, which had been
America's literary capital during the nineteenth century. Visiting New England for the first time, Cather was enchanted to
find herself in the region that had produced such renowned
writers as Nathaniel Hawthorne, Ralph Waldo Emerson, James
Russell Lowell, Oliver Wendell Holmes, and Henry
Wadsworth Longfellow. As a child in Red Cloud she had read
the works of all these men. She was even more impressed to
be introduced to Mrs. James T. Fields, an elderly widow whose
late husband had published those works at the famous Boston
publishing company Ticknor and Fields.

Many years later Cather described her meeting with Mrs.
Fields in the essay "148 Charles Street," whose title refers to
the Fieldses' address in Boston. During the nineteenth century
Mr. and Mrs. Fields had entertained many important authors—
not only the Americans whose works Ticknor and Fields published but also famous English visitors like Charles Dickens,

William Thackeray, and Matthew Arnold.

"For a period of sixty years," Cather wrote, the house on Charles Street had "extended its hospitality to the aristocracy of letters and art."[1] To be a guest in such a house was, for Cather, as divine an experience as one could imagine. There, she wrote, "an American of the Apache period and territory [meaning herself] could come to inherit a Colonial past."[2] For seven years, until Annie Fields's death in 1915, Cather returned periodically to her Charles Street parlor to listen to Mrs. Fields reminisce.

But the most important benefit of meeting Annie Fields was Cather's introduction to one of her friends, a noted writer from Maine named Sarah Orne Jewett. Cather had long admired Jewett's work, especially her collection of stories about the Maine coast called *The Country of the Pointed Firs* (1896). The two women liked each other immediately, and for more than a year they visited together often and exchanged letters. Jewett's sudden death in June 1909 at the age of sixty was a hard blow to Cather, and throughout her life she spoke often of how much Jewett's friendship had meant to her.

During their brief friendship Jewett had written and spoken many words of advice and encouragement. One line in particular stayed with Cather, and she quoted versions of it often in later life: "You must know the world before you can know the village."[3]

When Cather had been "discovered" by S. S. McClure in 1903, she had great hopes that the publisher's encouragement and influence would enable her to flourish as a writer of fiction. So far this had not happened. While there was great warmth and admiration between McClure and Cather, her duties at the magazine left little time to write short stories. In December 1908 she had celebrated her thirty-fifth birthday, and she was beginning to wonder if she would ever fulfill her dream of becoming a full-time writer.

In fact, Cather's literary output declined considerably during her years at *McClure's*. In 1907 she published four stories, but all of them had been written before she left Pittsburgh a year earlier. Another story appeared in 1908 and yet another in 1909, but she published nothing in 1910. Only in 1911, when she worked only nine months on the magazine, was she able to complete and publish a short story and also write a short novel.

Although most of the short stories that Cather published during this period were trivial and without lasting interest, one notable exception was "The Enchanted Bluff," which appeared in *Harper's Monthly* in April 1909. Set in Nebraska, it makes use of Cather's memories of camping on Far Island with her brothers and their friends. In the story a group of boys sit around a campfire while one of them tells an intriguing tale about a lost Indian village atop a bluff in New Mexico, "a big red rock . . . that goes right up out of the sand for about nine hundred feet."[4] Sixteenth-century Spanish explorers, led by Francisco de Coronado, also figure in the tale.

"The Enchanted Bluff" is considered another important milestone in Cather's literary career, for its Southwest setting as well as its use of Spanish history in the New World, both of which would play important roles in her later work. In this story, too, she uses a large rock (the bluff) as a symbol of history. Many years afterward the same symbol would appear in two of her most famous books: *Death Comes for the Archbishop* and *Shadows on the Rock*.

Concerned about her limited literary output, Cather confided her concerns about her future as a writer in letters to Sarah Orne Jewett during their sixteen-month friendship in 1908–1909. The daily grind of magazine editing left her exhausted every evening, Cather said, yet she was not sufficiently self-confident to give up the job. McClure himself did nothing to encourage her to write fiction; because he did not want to lose such an excellent employee, he tried to make her

As managing editor of McClure's Magazine *in New York City, Cather wore her most elegant clothes for this portrait by Fifth Avenue photographer Aimé Dupont. The tasseled jade necklace was a gift from the writer Sarah Orne Jewett, her friend and mentor.*

believe that she had no real future as a writer.

Jewett responded with sympathy and thoughtful comments about Cather's dilemma. She praised Cather's work thus far, in particular her story "The Sculptor's Funeral," and said that the aspiring writer had great potential. But she warned that unless Cather set aside "time and quiet" in order to "perfect" her talent, she would never mature as an artist. Cather's artistry was being hindered, Jewett said, by the demands of her job. She needed to find her own "quiet center of life, and write from that to the world."[5]

Following Jewett's advice was difficult for Cather to do, especially now that she was managing editor. Entrusted by McClure with enormous responsibility, she performed well and had the satisfaction of seeing circulation increase by 60,000 within a year. Cather traveled along the Eastern Seaboard seeking new stories for the magazine, and each spring McClure sent her to England to gather more material. Everywhere she went she met distinguished people—actors, statesmen, and others prominent in public life—as well as famous writers. Her position carried great prestige, especially for a woman, and she earned a generous salary. Deciding to leave such a life would have been very difficult for her.

In the end Cather did not have to make a choice; the decision was made for her. In the summer of 1911 McClure agreed to let her take a six-month vacation, beginning at the end of September. Despite a year of intermittent illness and an exhausting workload, Cather was in good spirits. Continued visits with Mrs. Fields, combined with several trips to see the Jewett family in South Berwick, Maine, undoubtedly produced a new surge of creativity in Cather. That summer she worked on a short story and her first novel, and looked forward to months of uninterrupted writing.

Changes in the fortunes of the McClure Company made her plans a certainty. The company had been experiencing financial difficulties for some time, despite the success of the magazine. That fall S. S. McClure lost control of his organization. New staff members were brought in, and Cather had to resign her position as managing editor. She would return briefly as a staff writer the following year, but in effect her career as a journalist was over.

Cather was nearly thirty-eight years old. Her long apprenticeship had been completed. Now, at last, she was free to enter the kingdom of art.

SEVEN

First Novel

Free at last of *McClure's* at the end of September 1911, Cather and her friend Isabelle McClung rented a cottage for three months in Cherry Valley, New York, a small village and health resort in rural Otsego County. McClung knew the area well. Her mother had grown up there, and she suggested it to Cather as a place where the writer could rest and work without interruption.

Otsego County was "Cooper country," the region where author James Fenimore Cooper had lived in the early nineteenth century and set most of his novels, including *The Last of the Mohicans*. Cather took little note of this, however; she had never expressed any liking for Cooper's books, and she intended to spend her time in Cherry Valley writing, not sightseeing.

For long hours each day, Cather sat at her desk with a bottle of ink, a dipping pen, and a pad of paper, writing. Her devoted friend McClung saw to it that she had adequate rest and quiet, and that meals, laundry, and cleaning were taken care of by a servant. However, as she would throughout her life whenever she found herself in a rural location, Cather took short breaks from her work schedule to hike in the countryside.

Her first order of business was revising the novel that she first called *Alexander's Masquerade* and then renamed

Alexander's Bridge. Cather later claimed that she wrote the novel during 1911, but no one knows exactly when she began work on it. How she managed to finish the first draft by September is a more intriguing question, given her serious illness, trip to England, and oppressive work schedule in the preceding eight months. Also surprising—because *McClure's* had bought so little of her work—is that the magazine agreed to publish the novel in installments in February, March, and April 1912.

During the time Cather spent in Boston in 1907 doing research on Mary Baker Eddy, she had met Ferris Greenslet, an editor at the publishing company Houghton Mifflin. Cather and the young editor became friends. When Greenslet learned that she had finally completed a novel, he encouraged her to send it to him. After completing her revisions in Cherry Valley, Cather mailed Greenslet a copy of *Alexander's Bridge.* It was quickly accepted by Houghton Mifflin, and Cather signed a contract on December 1, 1911, agreeing to publication in book form the following spring.

On the surface, Cather's first novel seems more closely related to some of her contrived early short stories than to her later books. For one thing, the story acquires its dramatic interest through a rather artificial, even hackneyed plot; this is not the gently unfolding narrative that would become her trademark. Moreover, its multiple settings include New York, Boston, London, and the St. Lawrence River in Quebec—but not Nebraska (although the reader does learn that the main character had grown up somewhere in the West).

Based on an actual disaster that occurred near Quebec City in 1907, *Alexander's Bridge* is the story of a structural engineer named Bartley Alexander. He is in his early forties and famous for building bridges. His current project is an enormous span across the St. Lawrence River in Canada. Alexander is married to a wealthy, socially prominent woman and appears happy to all who know him. However, his success has not brought him true contentment; he is restless and dissatisfied, looking for something in life that he can never find.

On a business trip to London, Alexander resumes a love affair with an actress, Hilda Burgoyne, whom he had known years earlier when he was a student in Paris. This, he thinks, will bring him the happiness he seeks. During the following year, as work on the great bridge goes forward, Alexander continues the affair in secret. Finally, he decides to leave his wife for Hilda, but his plans are interrupted when he learns that there are construction difficulties with the bridge. He hurries to Quebec, and as he inspects the structure it collapses into the river, killing Alexander and his workmen.

The symbolism in Cather's first novel seems obvious and even heavyhanded. Her main character is morally flawed, dishonest and dissatisfied, and this flaw is mirrored in his greatest accomplishment. His partly completed bridge, structurally unsound, "tore itself to pieces with roaring and grinding and noises that were like the shrieks of a steam whistle. . . . It lurched neither to right nor left, but sank almost in a vertical line, snapping and breaking and tearing as it went. . . ."[1]

But even though the plot seems simplistic, *Alexander's Bridge* expresses ideas that are important in Cather's later writing and also says something about her inner state of mind. As biographer James Woodress has noted, Bartley Alexander's "yearning and seeking for something he can't find"[2] is a theme in nearly all of Cather's fiction. So is a strong nostalgia for the past, in particular the "lost youth" that Alexander, like many of Cather's characters, is seeking.

Woodress, along with other critics, has noted that the tension in Cather's characters was her own as well. A strong dissatisfaction with the present, and an accompanying idealization of the past, would only intensify in both Cather and her work during the next three decades.

Alexander's Bridge did not bring Cather wider recognition and esteem, though it did receive favorable, if short, reviews in major magazines and newspapers, including the *New York Times*. Cather had long since turned her attention to writing several short stories, and for the rest of her life she dismissed her first novel as the work of a beginner.

Her three-month stay in Cherry Valley had been productive. After completing revisions of *Alexander's Bridge*, Cather had written a new story, "The Bohemian Girl," which she delightedly sold to *McClure's* for $500. She had also written most of another story, which she called "Alexandra," by the end of the year, when the cottage lease expired. She had planned to return to her apartment in New York City but became ill and was hospitalized for several weeks in Boston.

Periodic ill health now became a part of Cather's life and would continue until her death. Some of her ailments were specifically identified in letters to her friends, or later, in the memoirs that several of them wrote. Often, however, they remained mysteries, like her illness in 1912, which required surgery.

Some critics have wondered if there were psychological reasons for the recurring sicknesses that plagued Cather during the second half of her life and often required hospitalization for weeks at a time. A more obvious explanation can be found in her work habits: Cather approached every task with enormous energy, drive, and compulsion. Not surprisingly, exhaustion often resulted upon its completion, and Cather was then vulnerable to illness.

After leaving the hospital, Cather convalesced for several more weeks at a friend's home in Boston before returning to her apartment in late February. Now that she had recovered, she went ahead with plans for a trip she had been thinking of making for some time: a visit to the Southwest.

In early April 1912 Cather traveled west by train, stopping off briefly in Red Cloud to spend a few days with her family and friends before continuing her journey. The train eventually brought her to Winslow, Arizona, where her brother Douglas, who worked for the railroad, lived.

While Douglas was away supervising construction crews, Cather explored the nearby desert and canyons, led by a young Mexican named Julio. When Douglas returned, he took his sister on visits to Flagstaff, the Grand Canyon, and the ancient cliff dwellings at Walnut Canyon. Cather was emotionally stirred by the spectacular scenery, and by tales and legends of the old Southwest that she heard from Julio and others.

Like the Nebraska Divide, the Southwest would become another significant point on Willa Cather's literary compass.

Her imagination filled with ideas for new stories, Cather left Arizona in June and returned to Red Cloud. She stayed for five weeks, refreshing her memories of the Bohemian settlers on the Divide and watching them as they brought in their crops.

At the end of the summer, instead of returning to New York, Cather decided to go to the McClung house in Pittsburgh, where she was always welcomed. Back in her little converted sewing room on the third floor, watched over by Isabelle and freed from distractions, Cather began to write again.

EIGHT

Harvesting the Past

With the experience of the Divide, and the memories it had awakened, still fresh, Willa Cather sat down to write another short story set in pioneer Nebraska, which she called "The White Mulberry Tree." The story was based on an episode in Dante's fourteenth-century classic, *The Divine Comedy*, which Cather had first enjoyed reading as an adolescent. The episode tells of the tragic love affair between a married woman named Francesca and her friend Paolo.

In her rendering of the story, Cather transplanted the Italian lovers to the Nebraska prairie and re-created them as the Bohemian girl Marie Shabata and the Swedish farmer Emil Bergson. Marie's husband, Frank, comes upon them one evening, lying together under a white mulberry tree in his orchard, and he shoots them.

The idea for the story had come to Cather a few weeks earlier, as she stood on the edge of a Nebraska field and watched the farmers harvest wheat. She wrote it in just a few weeks and then compared it with "Alexandra," another story about the Divide that she had begun the previous winter in Cherry Valley. Cather realized immediately that the two stories belonged together, and that she could write more about these characters. Here were the makings of her second novel.

Cather's writing was interrupted twice that fall when *McClure's* called her back to New York to do temporary editorial work. Nevertheless, she was able to continue writing her new novel, which she named *O Pioneers!*, after the poem "Pioneers! O Pioneers!" by Walt Whitman. She had finished it by the end of the year and in early January 1913 returned with the manuscript to New York.

Set in the late nineteenth century on the Divide, near the fictional prairie town of Hanover (her pseudonym for Red Cloud), *O Pioneers!* tells the story of Alexandra Bergson, the daughter of Swedish immigrants, who passes up a chance for marriage in order to farm the land she inherits from her parents. The subplot is the tale of her youngest brother, Emil, and his love for Marie Shabata.

Alexandra struggles heroically and builds her stake into one of the best farms on the Divide. Her success is shadowed by her brother's love affair, which ends in tragedy under the mulberry tree. Alexandra's strength and fortitude are rewarded at the end of the novel, when her childhood sweetheart, Carl, returns and the two make plans to marry. Cather strengthens the flavor and interest of the narrative by incorporating numerous smaller stories about the lives of other immigrant pioneers on the Divide.

In fact, the Divide itself can be seen as a character in *O Pioneers!* "It seemed beautiful to her, rich and strong and glorious," Cather wrote, describing Alexandra's response to the landscape.

> *Her eyes drank in the breadth of it, until her tears blinded her. Then the Genius of the Divide, the great, free spirit which breathes across it, must have bent lower than it ever bent to a human will before. The history of every country begins in the heart of a man or a woman.*[1]

Cather sent the manuscript to Ferris Greenslet at Houghton Mifflin and it was promptly accepted. She signed a contract in late March, and *O Pioneers!* was published three months later.

Cather dedicated the book to the memory of her friend Sarah
Orne Jewett, who had encouraged her to write about those
things with which she was most familiar. Years earlier Jewett
had given her this advice in a letter: "The thing that teases
the mind over and over for years, and at last gets itself put
down rightly on paper—whether little or great, it belongs to
Literature."[2]

When Greenslet accepted *O Pioneers!* for publication, he
predicted that it would "definitely establish the author as a
novelist of the first rank." His prediction proved accurate. The
book was widely reviewed and almost uniformly praised. Critics especially lauded the poetic style Cather used to depict
both the glories and the hardships of life on the Divide. In
expressing her reverence for the immigrants who had settled
the West, Cather had contributed her own version of what
became an American myth: that the country's greatest glory
lay in its pioneer past. This myth of a glorious past would
appear in all of Cather's major fiction.

Cather had now resettled in New York City, in the new apartment she shared with Edith Lewis at 5 Bank Street in Greenwich Village. She continued to do free-lance work—editing
and writing drama reviews—for *McClure's* because she needed
the income. During June and July she also was the ghostwriter
for S. S. McClure's autobiography. The written work was
entirely hers, based on McClure's reminiscences during weekly
visits to her apartment.

McClure, born in 1857, was a self-made Irish immigrant
who had become the most influential editor of his time;
despite his recent financial troubles, he continued to be
respected for his accomplishments. *My Autobiography* was serialized in *McClure's* in 1913–1914, then published in book form.
Told in a simple, straightforward style, the autobiography was
enormously popular and became a best-seller.

Although the book included a note by McClure thanking

Cather for her "assistance," the fact that she wrote it herself was widely known. Unlike her attitude toward the Mary Baker Eddy biography, Cather openly acknowledged her authorship. Cather was extremely fond of McClure, with whom she remained friends throughout her life, and was happy to be of assistance to him at a time when his fortunes were low. The book helped her former boss psychologically as well as financially, but it is unlikely that Cather regarded it as anything more than a piece of journalism, like her earlier work on Mary Baker Eddy.

Cather took on other projects for *McClure's* in 1913. One was a long article, "Training for the Ballet," which described the ballet school at the Metropolitan Opera; it appeared in the October issue. Another was "Three American Singers," a profile of Metropolitan Opera stars Louise Homer, Geraldine Farrar, and Olive Fremstad that was published in December.

Cather had become an enthusiastic operagoer after moving to New York. She frequently attended performances at the Metropolitan Opera House, then located at 39th Street and Broadway, riding the north-bound trolley with Edith Lewis from their Greenwich Village apartment. One of her favorite singers was Olive Fremstad, a Swedish-born soprano who had grown up in Minnesota and specialized in the operas of the German composer Richard Wagner. Cather was thrilled when she was granted an interview with Fremstad in the spring of 1913, and out of their first meeting a strong friendship developed.

Cather found much to admire in Fremstad, who had struggled for many years to gain her status as the Met's leading Wagnerian soprano. She believed that Fremstad resembled the strong Swedish pioneer women of the Divide, who resolutely fought all obstacles to establish their families. Cather also saw something of herself in Fremstad: the opera singer was a kindred spirit, an artist who had strived to achieve a name for herself. As she watched Fremstad sing, exchanged letters, and visited at Fremstad's apartment and at her cottage in Maine, Cather grew increasingly certain that she had found the subject for her next novel.

Willa Cather dedicated The Song of the Lark *to Isabelle McClung, her dearest friend. McClung, a Pittsburgh socialite, shared her home with Cather and acted as her muse.*

Cather still believed that she could write fiction best in her old room at the McClung house in Pittsburgh. Following a visit with Isabelle to Back Creek Valley, Virginia, in late summer 1913, she lived in October and November at the McClungs and was able to make a good start on her new book. Then another journalistic assignment called her back to New York.

During the next six months, Cather did very little actual writing on her book, although she continued to gather information about the world of opera as further background material. She paid close attention to Fremstad, the model for the book's heroine, whom Cather had named Thea Kronborg.

Between articles for *McClure's* Cather hoped to get back to her manuscript, but that winter she was felled by another illness, this time severe blood poisoning caused by a scratch from a hatpin. She had to spend three weeks in the hospital, then more than a month recuperating at home, and she became severely depressed. Olive Fremstad visited her often, bringing flowers to cheer her.

In May Cather went back to Pittsburgh for several more weeks of work on the novel, then traveled to Maine to spend time with Fremstad at her cottage. That summer she made an extended visit to Nebraska and the Southwest, refreshing her memory of places and people that she wanted to use in her book. By late September of 1914, as World War I raged in Europe, she was back in her study at the McClungs'. For the next five and a half months, Cather worked on the novel that she had decided to call *The Song of the Lark*.

Cather named the book after a well-known painting by the same title that she had seen during a visit to Chicago's Art Institute. The painting shows a French peasant girl in a field pausing to listen to a lark singing. The title, she later explained, was supposed to "suggest a young girl's awakening to something beautiful,"[3] but most readers missed the allusion, believing instead that it was a direct reference to the larklike voice of the book's heroine.

By February 1915 Cather had nearly finished *The Song of the Lark*, and she returned to New York to complete it. At the end of March she sent the manuscript to Ferris Greenslet at Houghton Mifflin, confident that she had written her best book yet. Greenslet, however, had doubts about the novel, which he thought was too long and somewhat disconnected in its plot structure. He suggested revisions, some of which Cather agreed to make.

In the following weeks editor and author worked together, though not always happily, for Cather was disappointed at Greenslet's lack of enthusiasm. Cather hoped that the book would become a best-seller and earn her a fair amount of money, thus freeing her forever from having to accept freelance journalism assignments.

By late spring the book was in production and scheduled for publication in October. Cather spent a number of weeks reading and correcting galley proofs, and by August she was ready for a vacation. Accompanied by Edith Lewis—her usual traveling companion, Isabelle McClung, had to remain at home caring for her ailing father—Cather traveled west by train to visit Mesa Verde National Park, in southwestern Colorado.

Prehistoric cliff dwellings, the most extensive in the United States, had been discovered at Mesa Verde in 1888; a national park had been created on the site eighteen years later. Cather had been eager to visit Mesa Verde ever since her first trip to Colorado in 1912, when the ruins at Walnut Canyon had stirred her imagination. She and Lewis camped in a tent at the park and spent a week exploring the cliffs. Cather was an enthusiastic hiker, horseback rider, and camper, and as always the observant writer was recording impressions for future use.

Toward the end of the visit, on a trip into an unexplored canyon, their guide lost his way and left the women while he went for help. The experience did not faze Cather in the slightest; as the day ended and twilight came, Cather and Lewis settled themselves on a large rock and watched the moon rise over the canyon rim. When rescuers finally appeared early the following morning, Cather was astounded to learn that her "disappearance" had been reported to the news media. She had never doubted for a moment, she said, that they would be found. The incident was written about in newspapers throughout the country, including the *New York Times*.[4]

After her stay in Mesa Verde, Cather spent a week in Taos, New Mexico, then a remote settlement in the Sangre de Cristo Mountains along the Santa Fe Trail. As she had on her earlier visit to the Southwest, Cather was enchanted by the countryside and enjoyed "roughing it," staying in a primitive inn and exploring the area on horseback. In mid-September she traveled northeast to Red Cloud and settled in for a long visit. Cather was still there on October 2, 1915, when *The Song of the Lark* was published in Boston, more than 1,500 miles away.

Cather's third novel chronicles the development of a musical artist. Part I, "The Friends of Childhood," is set in the fictional prairie town of Moonstone, Colorado (another version of Red Cloud), in the 1880s and describes the growing-up years of young Thea Kronborg. Cather draws heavily on her own childhood experiences as she describes Thea's growth into adolescence, and many of the characters are variations of people she knew in Red Cloud. As the novel progresses, she makes increasing use of Olive Fremstad's experiences, too. Cather later remarked that the two women's stories were so intertwined in the novel that she could not say exactly where one ended and the other began.

Central to Thea's life is Dr. Archie, the family physician, who appears throughout the book and is modeled on several of Cather's childhood doctors. Archie is childless and, like so many of Cather's fictional characters, unhappily married. A strong bond develops between Thea and Archie. He becomes her mentor and confidant, and encourages her musical talent. When Thea inherits money from a friend, Archie urges her to continue her studies in Chicago, where he finds her a teacher, a place to live, and a job as soloist with a church choir. Part II traces Thea's artistic unfolding and her discovery that her voice is her greatest talent. When she returns to Moonstone for summer vacation, she realizes that she no longer has much in common with her old friends; she has established an independent life.

In Part III Thea continues her voice studies in Chicago while she supports herself by church singing and accompanying her teacher's other pupils. She works hard but becomes exhausted and discouraged at her seeming lack of progress. Help appears in the form of wealthy Fred Ottenburg, an amateur musician, who offers her the use of the family ranch in Arizona for a summer vacation.

In Part IV Thea travels to Panther Canyon—a fictional version of Walnut Canyon. Rest and relaxation and inspiring scenery bring about her rebirth, and she decides to go to Germany for further study. However, when Fred joins her at the ranch, a romance develops between them and Thea believes that they will be married. She travels to Mexico City with Fred, then discovers that he is already married—unhappily— and cannot get a divorce from his wife.

Renouncing Fred, Thea resumes her plan to study in Germany. In Part V she borrows money from Dr. Archie and prepares to go abroad. Part VI takes place a decade later. Thea is now a leading soprano at the Metropolitan Opera after establishing a successful career, like Fremstad, in Germany. In a brief epilogue the reader learns that Thea later marries the widowed Fred Ottenburg. Her professional victory has been won at great personal cost, for she is wed primarily to her art and must work relentlessly to maintain perfection.

Yet Thea believes that no other choice was possible, for she was born an artist and must give herself to the development of her art. "Artistic growth is, more than it is anything else, a refining of the sense of truthfulness," Cather writes of her heroine, and "only the artist, the great artist, knows how difficult it is."[5] As the mature Thea explains to Fred Ottenburg, she has come to recognize and accept "the inevitable hardness of human life. No artist gets far who doesn't know that. And you can't know it with your mind. You have to realize it in your body; deep."[6]

Cather received praise for *The Song of the Lark* from many influential critics, and she was pleased most of all with Fremstad's ecstatic reaction to the book. However, it did not sell as many copies as she had hoped, and she blamed Houghton Mifflin for not marketing it vigorously. Cather was also disappointed when William Heinemann, a British publisher who had issued an English edition of *O Pioneers!*, refused to publish her third novel.

Heinemann thought the book was too long—it was three times the length of *O Pioneers!*—and had unnecessary detail. Even some of Cather's most appreciative critics made the same comment, and many years later Cather herself agreed. Perhaps

Ferris Greenslet had been right in asking for cuts that she had refused. But in 1932, when she prepared a new edition of *The Song of the Lark*, Cather made only minor deletions. The book should remain largely the same, she decided—as an accurate expression of her artistic self in the year 1915.

NINE

The Triumph of Memory

W illa Cather now stood on the threshold of a great career. But like the fictional Thea Kronborg on the eve of her greatest success, Cather could not help feeling discouraged as the year 1916 began.

For one thing, *The Song of the Lark* was not selling as well as she had hoped, so her royalties were relatively small. (A royalty is a percentage of a book's earnings that is paid by the publisher to the author.) Most of the handful of women who pursued careers in the arts in the early twentieth century came from wealthy backgrounds and were given living allowances by their families; they did not have to depend upon their creative output for rent and food. For example, Edith Wharton, another leading American novelist of the period, had a sizable inherited fortune to rely on. Cather, on the other hand, had to support herself, and she also felt obligated to send money to her large family.

Cather lived modestly, but ever since graduating from college she had been helping to finance the education of her brothers and sisters. She had also been a generous contributor to relief funds for war refugees, and continued what became her lifelong habit of helping out friends who were hard up.

Cather had been relieved when her article assignments

from *McClure's* ended, but she still needed the regular income that they provided. Instead of journalistic reviews and profiles, she now wrote short stories that were bought by magazines for as much as $600 apiece, thanks to the efforts of Paul Reynolds, who had become her agent. Cather believed that she had outgrown short fiction, however; what she really wanted to do was write novels, and she disliked the distraction of having to turn out stories quickly to earn money.

Her personal life at this time was also troubling to Cather. Judge McClung had died the previous November, and Cather spent her last Christmas in Pittsburgh at the McClung house. Early in 1916 the house was sold, in effect ending her twenty-year association with the city. This was a large blow to Cather, who had looked upon the McClung residence as a real home and the site of her best writing. Less than a year earlier she had also mourned the death of Annie Fields in Boston and the loss of that household, too.

Another blow followed: Isabelle McClung, freed from looking after her father, announced her engagement to a concert violinist named Jan Hambourg. Cather was devastated; she believed that she was now losing her dearest, closest friend. Nevertheless, she managed to pull herself together enough to help Isabelle plan the wedding, which was held in New York in April. The couple lived in the city for a while after their marriage, and as Cather saw more of Jan she became less resentful. The friendship between the two women continued for more than two decades, and during that time Cather visited frequently with the Hambourgs. But Cather believed that a precious part of her life was now over.

Now in her forty-third year of life, Willa Cather was entering middle age. As if her own personal turmoil were not hard enough to bear, the daily newspapers brought horrifying accounts of the savage war in Europe. Recollections of earlier times came flooding back to her, years when the world seemed a brighter, happier place. An idea was stirring inside her for a new novel, set in the Southwest, a region she had grown to love. As soon as her financial circumstances allowed, she planned to begin work on it.

Meanwhile, there were other friends in New York to see. Sometime in the spring of 1916 Cather began holding a weekly open house on Friday afternoons at her Bank Street apartment. These open houses became a genuine source of pleasure for her and continued into the 1920s, until her fame attracted more people than Cather and her small living room could handle.

In the summer of 1916 Cather traveled west again, visiting first Denver and then Taos, where she spent three weeks riding horseback in the mountains. Then she went on to Wyoming to stay for a while with her married brother Roscoe and his family. At the end of August, Cather returned to the family home in Red Cloud for a visit that continued for three months. Her mother was ill, and Cather took over her duties as cook and housekeeper. Earlier during summer vacation she had managed to write and sell several short stories, but in Red Cloud family responsibilities limited her to sporadic work on a tale set in the Southwest that she called "The Blue Mesa."

One day that fall, Cather hitched up the family horse-and-buggy and drove out to the Divide, to the region called "Bohemian country," to visit her old friend Annie Sadilek Pavelka. Annie, now married to a farmer, had become the mother of ten children as exuberant and full of joy as their mother. Annie's obvious pride in her large family was a glorious sight, and the experience moved Cather deeply. Memories of the childhood Annie overwhelmed Cather and forced her to put aside work on "The Blue Mesa" as well as plans for a novel about the Southwest. An idea for a new novel had formed. It would be about Nebraska, and its heroine would be a young woman like Annie Sadilek Pavelka. She would call it *My Ántonia*.

*A latecomer as a novelist, Cather was in her mid-forties before her fiction
attracted wide recognition. On a trip home to Nebraska—possibly in 1917,
to receive an honorary doctorate, her first, from the university—Cather
wore a favorite jacket from the Southwest for this photograph taken at a
Lincoln studio.*

Cather began writing her new novel as soon as she returned to
New York at Thanksgiving. For the time being, income from
short stories that Reynolds had sold allowed her to work on it
full-time. By early spring of 1917 she had completed at least
half of a first draft and hoped then to finish by June. Despite
her rigorous daily writing schedule, however, Cather found
that she could not make this deadline. Somehow she seemed
to linger far more over the raw materials for this novel than
she had in writing her earlier books. There were so many
memories to be sorted through, examined carefully, and re-
created into art.

And Cather was taking time to have an enjoyable social
life, too. Visits to the opera, concerts, and art museums contin-

ued, and her Friday-afternoon receptions flourished. That spring she visited Washington, D.C., again, then traveled west to receive her first honorary degree—from her alma mater, the University of Nebraska—and vacationed with her brother Roscoe in Wyoming.

Summer breaks were essential to Cather, but she always returned from them impatient and eager to resume writing. However, she believed that the Bank Street apartment she shared with Edith Lewis was not an ideal place for her creativity to flourish. She needed to separate herself from everyday distractions at another haven, a place like her sewing-room study at the McClung house in Pittsburgh. She found her new refuge at the Shattuck Inn in Jaffrey, New Hampshire.

Cather had visited the White Mountains of New Hampshire during her first trip to New England, in 1907. The Hambourgs were staying at the Shattuck Inn in the late summer of 1917 and they invited Cather to come see them in September, after she had returned from her western trip. Cather brought the manuscript for *My Ántonia* with her, hoping to work on it. She found the area so congenial that she stayed for nearly two months. As long as weather permitted, she did her writing outdoors, in a small tent pitched in a nearby meadow.

The novel was still unfinished when Cather returned to New York in late October. Again, because she needed the money, Cather had to put the novel aside briefly while she turned out more short fiction. In recent years these stories had been mostly about musicians and artists. This time she wrote several stories about life in a magazine publishing office, based largely on her experiences at *McClure's*. As soon as she could, Cather resumed work on *My Ántonia*, sending it bit by bit to Ferris Greenslet at Houghton Mifflin.

The writing was still going slowly, in part because Cather was forced to stay at the Bank Street apartment to work. Because of wartime fuel shortages, she had no coal to heat her study and suffered a severe attack of bronchitis in February. Olive Fremstad again came to her rescue, bringing Cather to her apartment by chauffeur-driven limousine for dinner and musical entertainments. Cather was also cheered by her other friends, including the Hambourgs, and by her Friday-afternoon gatherings, which resumed as her health improved.

Finally, during the third week of June 1918, Cather sent the last pages of *My Ántonia* to Ferris Greenslet, then returned to the Shattuck Inn in Jaffrey for a working vacation. As each chapter was set into type, Greenslet sent Cather galley proofs for her corrections. By the end of July Cather had corrected all the galleys. She was back in Red Cloud with her family that fall when her fourth novel was published.

My Ántonia could be described as both biographical and autobiographical fiction. Its heroine is a Bohemian immigrant girl named Ántonia Shimerda, whose life story closely parallels that of Annie Sadilek Pavelka. It is also the autobiography of the novel's narrator, Jim Burden, who had grown up with Ántonia in the fictional town of Black Hawk (Red Cloud). Jim is a thinly disguised version of Willa Cather, and the youthful experiences he recalls are similar to her own.

My Ántonia is told in the form of a memoir: the adult Jim, a graduate of Harvard University and now a successful lawyer in New York, recalls growing up in Nebraska and his attraction to the older Ántonia, who works as a hired girl for a neighboring family. Even after leaving Nebraska to go east to college, Burden still thinks about Ántonia. Over the years he hears from friends and relatives about her experiences, both happy and sad, as she progresses into an ultimately contented maturity.

Among all the heroines that Cather created, Ántonia Shimerda was probably her favorite. During the winter of 1916–1917, when Cather was working intensively on the novel's early chapters, she revealed her feelings about Ántonia—and Annie Pavelka, whom she represented—to a close friend, a journalist named Elizabeth Shepley Sergeant.

As Sergeant recalls in her memoir of Cather, the author arrived at Sergeant's apartment for tea one afternoon in midwinter, following a brisk walk in Central Park. Her cheeks were glowing, her eyes sparkling, as she spoke to Sergeant about her novel. Suddenly Cather jumped up and seized a rare ceramic jar, glazed in shades of orange and blue and filled with dried orange-brown flowers. She placed it in the middle of a bare round antique table.

"I want my new heroine to be like this," Cather said, "like a rare object in the middle of a table, which one may examine from all sides." She moved a lamp close to the table so that the colors of the jar glinted. "I want her to stand out—like this—like this," she added, "because she *is* the story."[1]

In the book Cather describes Ántonia as having eyes that were

big and warm and full of light, like the sun shining on brown pools in the wood. Her skin was brown, too, and in her cheeks she had a glow of rich, dark colour. Her brown hair was curly and wild-looking.[2]

Although the focus of the novel is always on Ántonia, we learn about Jim Burden's early experiences as well, experiences that are also Cather's. Burden/Cather and Ántonia/Annie have traveled different roads to adulthood, Burden concludes, but they have in common "the precious, the incommunicable past."[3]

Above all, *My Ántonia* is a hymn to the past, to a Golden Age whose heroes and heroines were immigrant men, women, and children who together tamed the rebellious prairie into fertile farmland, overcoming fierce storms and droughts, poisonous snakes, and hostile Indians. Ántonia Shimerda Cuzak herself is a metaphor for the fertility of the land:

She had only to stand in the orchard, to put her hand on a little crab tree and look up at the apples, to make you feel the goodness of planting and tending and harvesting at last. . . . She was a rich mine of life, like the founders of early races.[4]

Near the end of the novel, in one of its most memorable scenes, Jim Burden describes his visit as a middle-aged man to the Cuzak farm. Ántonia and her numerous children take him to see their "fruit cave," a cellar where she stores jars of preserved strawberries, cherries, and crab apples. Jim climbs back outside with Ántonia and watches as the children come running out, "big and little, tow heads and gold heads and brown, and flashing little naked legs; a veritable explosion of life out of the dark cave into the sunlight."[5]

Woven into the narrative are stories and characters that Cather remembered from childhood, including the suicide of Francis Sadilek, Annie's real-life father, who is fictionalized as Mr. Shimerda, Ántonia's father, in the novel. The suicide had been the subject of Cather's first published short story, "Peter," written in 1891 during her freshman year at the University of Nebraska.

My Ántonia received glowing reviews from critics, who called it a major contribution to American literature, but Cather was disappointed when it failed to become a best-seller. World War I had ended in the fall of 1918, not long after its publication, and public attention was focused on getting back to normal after several years of food and fuel shortages. The novel sold moderately well—8,000 copies during the first year—but Cather's royalties for that same year totaled a modest $2,000. This was barely enough to support her while she wrote another novel, but she would have to make do.

Cather already knew the next book she wanted to write. It would be about Nebraska, but it would also be about the war that had just ended. Perhaps this would be the book, she thought, that would capture the public imagination in a way that her first four novels had so far not been able to do.

TEN

Popular Acclaim

The idea for her fifth novel had formed in Willa Cather's mind in the early fall of 1918, during the weeks she spent at home in Red Cloud. One afternoon she had gone to visit Aunt Franc—Frances Cather, the wife of her father's brother George—at her farm home on the Divide. Aunt Franc's only son, called G.P., had been killed the previous spring while fighting with the American Expeditionary Force in France. His mother had kept all the letters he had written home, and Cather sat for several hours reading through them.

Cather had played with young G.P. during her brief residence at Catherton and later, after she had moved into Red Cloud. The cousins had drifted apart as they grew older, and while Willa had gone on to the university and a career in the East, G.P. had tried to make a life for himself as a farmer, without much success. She had last seen him several years earlier, during a visit to Nebraska. G.P. was a quiet man who found it difficult to express his frustration directly, but he had barely concealed his resentment at Willa's "escape" from the prairie and his unfulfilled desire to live what he imagined was a more exciting, glamorous life.

Willa Cather remained fond of her cousin, despite his bitterness, and expressed pleasure when he enlisted in the army.

Great patriotic fervor had erupted when the United States entered World War I in 1917. Many people, in the words of President Woodrow Wilson, saw the war as a battle to "make the world safe for democracy." Cather thought that military service abroad would give her cousin G.P. the chance to experience, however briefly, a glorious and dramatic moment in world history and might pull him out of the doldrums. G.P. received a citation for bravery shortly before he was killed, and she mourned his death in battle as the splendid last act of a hero.

Reading his letters inspired Cather to make up a story about a similar young man who had grown up on the Nebraska prairie. She named her character Claude Wheeler and for a while she called the novel "Claude." Only after she had been working on it for several years did she rename it *One of Ours.*

Cather began writing her new novel soon after returning to New York in the fall of 1918 and worked on it steadily during the following months at her Bank Street apartment and later in Jaffrey, New Hampshire. To learn more about army life so that she could reproduce it authentically in her novel, Cather talked with Nebraska soldiers who were passing through New York on their way home from France. Friends brought some of them to her apartment to be interviewed; she visited others at a military hospital in the city.

"Claude" took even longer to write than *My Ántonia* had, but Cather did not feel pressured to rush to complete it. A major factor in her more leisurely attitude was an improvement in her financial situation. Not only were royalties on the American editions of her first four novels coming in steadily; she had also received money from the sale of her novels to several publishers abroad and now began to collect royalties from the sale of foreign-language editions.

In December 1919 Cather took a break from "Claude" to write a short story called "Coming, Aphrodite!" She did it purely for pleasure, she told friends, and was further delighted when her agent sold it to the sophisticated magazine *Smart Set*. "Coming, Aphrodite!" was a crisply written tale of a struggling painter living in Greenwich Village and his brief love affair with an aspiring singer. When the story was well-received by readers, Cather decided to combine it with other tales she had written about artists and musicians, including four of the stories in *The Troll Garden*, and publish the collection as *Youth and the Bright Medusa*.

During the past two years, Cather had become increasingly dissatisfied with her publisher, Houghton Mifflin. She complained to Ferris Greenslet that the company did not try hard enough to sell her books, and that it charged her too much for corrections she made on galley proofs. Houghton Mifflin published many well-known authors, and Cather did not think the company regarded her work highly enough. Meanwhile, other publishing companies had begun to express an interest in her writing.

Cather was especially impressed with a young publisher named Alfred A. Knopf, who had founded a company under his own name in 1915. Knopf had a talent for promoting books, and Cather was flattered when he expressed admiration for her work. Although she had an agreement with Houghton Mifflin for the publication of what became *One of Ours*, she accepted an offer from Knopf to publish *Youth and the Bright Medusa*.

When it was published in 1920, *Youth and the Bright Medusa* sold steadily, thanks to Knopf's promotion. Cather made as much money from it in six months as she did in twice that time from *My Ántonia*. Knopf assured her that she would become a major American author and that he would work hard to sell all her books. Impressed, Cather ended her relationship with Houghton Mifflin and agreed to let Knopf publish *One of Ours* upon its completion.

Thus began an association that lasted until the end of Cather's life. Knopf became not only her publisher but a warm and valued personal friend as well, together with his wife and co-founder, Blanche. Knopf's fortunes and Cather's quickly grew together, and in the late twentieth century the company he founded continues to flourish.

The spring of 1920 found Cather still at work on *One of Ours*. She decided that before she wrote about Claude's experiences in France she had to visit the country and learn more about it. She had not been there since her first trip abroad with Isabelle McClung in 1902.

In late May 1920 Cather and Edith Lewis sailed abroad for a six-month stay. They spent more than a month in Paris, and Cather, along with Isabelle McClung Hambourg, made a visit during this time to G.P. Cather's grave near Cantigny, some sixty miles north of the French capital. Then Cather joined both Hambourgs for a tour of southern France that was cut short when she became ill. The trio settled in Cavalière, a small fishing village on the Mediterranean, while Cather recuperated and worked on her novel.

There was good news for Cather when she returned to the United States in November: *Youth and the Bright Medusa* was selling briskly and had received enthusiastic reviews from leading critics. At last she had both a popular and a critical success to her credit. But she still had *One of Ours* to finish. She worked continually on the manuscript and at the end of August 1921 sent the finished work to Knopf. It had taken her nearly three years to write, longer than any of her other books.

Tired but relieved, Cather arrived in Red Cloud in September to find herself the center of a great deal of attention. The reason for her newfound celebrity was a talk given that summer in Omaha by American author Sinclair Lewis, who had become famous after writing his satirical, best-selling novel *Main Street* (1920). Lewis praised Cather's work and hailed her as Nebraska's leading citizen because of her sympathetic depictions of pioneer life.

That fall Cather gave speeches and interviews in several

Nebraska towns and cities, including Lincoln and Omaha. She returned to New York in early November after stopping in Chicago for more speechmaking, more interviews, and a tour of the city's leading bookstores to promote her books.

After such a full schedule Cather, not surprisingly, became ill again. This time she experienced digestive problems and consulted a stomach specialist in New York City, who prescribed a special diet. Cather gradually recovered that winter and resumed her active social life, but by early spring she was ill with tonsillitis and had to have her tonsils removed. Exhausted from the illness and surgery, she recuperated for several weeks at a sanitarium in rural Wernersville, Pennsylvania.

Cather was able to correct proofs for *One of Ours* as she grew stronger, and she was still working on them after her return to New York in May. Two months later, in July 1922, with all proofs corrected and her health restored, Cather traveled to Middlebury, Vermont, to give a series of lectures at Bread Loaf, an annual summer school for aspiring writers.

Cather had gotten the job through the recommendation of an old Nebraska friend, the former Dorothy Canfield. Now married and known as Dorothy Canfield Fisher, she lived in Vermont and had published several novels. Cather had taken the job because she needed the money—she was paid $1,000 for five lectures—but she did not believe that "creative" writing could be taught. Cather felt that all students should receive a firm grounding in English grammar and sentence structure, but literary talent could not be acquired in a classroom. Bread Loaf was her first teaching experience since leaving Pittsburgh in 1906, and it became her last.

In August Cather continued north via train to New Brunswick, Canada, and discovered a place that became her new summer home: the island of Grand Manan, near the coast of Maine in the Bay of Fundy. Cather had heard about Grand Manan several years earlier from a librarian friend in New York, who recommended it as an ideal retreat for a writer. The island was isolated and sparsely settled, and Cather could work there without interruption. She rented a cottage in the small fishing village of Whale Cove and began revising the short story "The Blue Mesa," which she had begun in 1916. Retitled "Tom Outland's Story," it would become a significant part of her next novel.

In September 1922, while Cather was writing at Whale Cove, *One of Ours* was published in the United States. Cather's fifth novel covers six years in the life of Claude Wheeler, beginning at the age of nineteen on a Nebraska farm. Wheeler has a sensitive, artistic temperament, and he finds the coarseness of farm life repulsive. Thinking that marriage will give him a sense of purpose, he weds a woman who soon rejects him. To escape from this meaningless existence, he joins the army and is sent to France.

There Wheeler finds a world of art and beauty, and his spirit is reborn. He becomes friendly with another soldier, a college-educated American violinist named David Gerhardt. Gerhardt is fluent in French and acts as Wheeler's guide to the country's culture and its people. Wheeler celebrates his twenty-fifth birthday with a local family and realizes that for the first time he is completely happy. "Life had after all turned out well for him," the narrator writes, "and everything had a noble significance. The nervous tension in which he had lived for years now seemed incredible to him. . . . He was beginning over again."[1]

Not long afterward, Wheeler and his friend Gerhardt are killed in action on the same day. In an epilogue, Wheeler's mother back in Nebraska continues to receive letters from her son written before his death. She is comforted by the knowledge that his months overseas were happy. She even feels relieved that Wheeler did not have to return to America to live, for she believes that he would have been saddened by the increasing materialism of postwar society.

Cather was disappointed when *One of Ours* received negative reviews from leading literary critics. Many believed that as a woman she had failed to write convincingly about war. Others complained that the book was overly long (459 pages in the first edition) and tedious to read. Still others objected to Claude Wheeler's portrayal as a hero in battle, saying that instead Cather should have created a more realistic character by making Wheeler cynical and disillusioned by warfare. What these critics missed—and what later critics and readers have discovered—is Cather's irony: Wheeler experiences the "noble significance" of life in a country that is being destroyed in a devastating conflict.

There were a small number of favorable reviews of *One of Ours* in 1922, but they were written by less influential critics and by some of her friends. Dorothy Canfield Fisher, for example, praised *One of Ours* in the *New York Times*.

The book may not have been a critical success but the public loved it. In the first month after publication, 16,000 copies were sold; in twelve months, 54,000. Cather had written a best-seller that earned her $19,000 in royalties in the first year of publication. The success of *One of Ours* also led to increased sales of her other books. Her money worries were now over.

And the negative critics were squelched in the spring of 1923, when Cather received America's most prestigious literary award: the Pulitzer Prize for writing what the judges considered the best novel of 1922.

ELEVEN

A Search for Meaning

This should have been the happiest time of Willa Cather's life. Her longtime goal had been achieved: she was a nationally recognized writer of fiction. Moreover, she was now financially secure; no longer would she have to do work solely for money.

Yet Cather was discontented. Dissatisfaction and impatience had long been prominent characteristics of her personality, but such feelings could be explained as the natural frustrations of a talented woman seeking recognition. Now there had to be another explanation for Cather's depression.

There *were* several reasons why she might have felt dejected: For one thing, her beloved friend Isabelle McClung Hambourg had now settled permanently in Europe with her husband, and Cather feared that their relationship would be confined mostly to letters. For another, she was having trouble accepting the harsh criticism leveled against *One of Ours*, despite its popularity. As someone who wished to be known as an artist, Cather must have suffered acutely at this time from hurt pride.

Yet the impact of both of these events had been softened. In the case of Isabelle, Cather had had several years to get used to a change in their relationship following her friend's marriage. As for hostile reviews of *One of Ours*, Cather had the consolation of enormous royalties and, later, the Pulitzer Prize.

Cather herself must have been both puzzled and dismayed by her feelings at this time. After all, she had little tolerance for her many bouts of illness and always criticized them as "weaknesses" in letters to friends. On the surface Cather tried to maintain an air of composure, for she abhorred emotional outbursts as much as she disliked her physical ailments. Only years later, in an introductory note to a collection of essays, did she allude briefly to her mental anguish in the early 1920s: "The world broke in two in 1922 or thereabouts," she wrote in *Not Under Forty* (1936).[1]

What Willa Cather was suffering from was, and continues to be, a common problem. Only in the late twentieth century have psychologists given it a name: *midlife crisis*. The term describes the feelings of anxiety that often accompany the onset of middle age. These feelings are believed to be a psychological response to changes in one's life. At this time, men may mourn the loss of their youth as they realize they are growing older and losing physical strength. By the age of fifty, most women have entered menopause, which ends their ability to have children.

When human beings are under stress, they may feel a profound personal connection to unpleasant events in the outside world, even when these events have no direct bearing on their own lives. This is probably what happened to Willa Cather in 1922, when "the world broke in two."

By the time Cather turned forty-nine, in December 1922, a deep pessimism had spread in the Western world among educated, serious-thinking men and women. Four years after the armistice that halted World War I, it was clear that the world had not been made "safe for democracy." As the League of Nations struggled for existence—the United States refused to join—foreign governments still wrangled over financial settlements, boundary disputes, and territorial claims.

Meanwhile, in an effort to ignore Europe's problems, much of the United States had erupted into what would become a decade-long orgy of materialism known as the "Roaring Twenties." With the manufacture and sale of alcoholic beverages banned by the 18th Amendment to the U.S. Constitution in 1919, bootlegging and speakeasies flourished as millions of Americans were caught up in a frenzied pursuit of wealth and leisure.

For a woman and an artist like Willa Cather, this was a time to look backward to the last century, when honest labor, not greed, had created an age of peace and simple comforts on the American prairie. This was not a new thought for Cather, of course. In *My Ántonia* she had movingly celebrated the past, and in *One of Ours* Claude Wheeler had been unhappy with changes in farm life: the former sense of community had broken down as the sons of pioneers became "either stingy and grasping, or extravagant and lazy."[2]

Now, as her own midlife crisis and the nation's coincided, Cather used her gifts to transform anguish into art. Out of the acute tension between her reverence for an idealized past and her disillusionment with the present would come some of her finest writing.

Up until now, Willa Cather would not have described herself as a religious person. As a child she had attended the Baptist church in Red Cloud, but by the time she was a college student in Lincoln, Cather characterized herself as an atheist.

In middle age her feelings toward religion apparently changed. How this came about is not known, but it was obviously a response to the dejection she had been feeling. Later she would say only that "faith is a gift"[3] but make no further comment. An acknowledgment of this new religious faith came two days after Christmas in 1922.

Cather had returned to Red Cloud after Thanksgiving to celebrate her parents' golden wedding anniversary. The entire family gathered for the event in early December, and it proved to be a joyous occasion. Cather was pleased to see her parents enjoying good health, and visits to the immigrant settlements on the Divide refreshed her. Shortly before returning to New York, on December 27, 1922, she was confirmed, along with her parents, as an Episcopalian in a private ceremony at Red Cloud's Grace Church.

For the rest of her life Cather maintained her membership in Grace Church and helped support it financially. In New York City she attended the Church of the Transfiguration on East 29th Street; also known as "the Little Church Around the Corner," it was then—and continues to be—an Episcopal parish for New Yorkers who are active in the arts.

Despite her inner turmoil, 1922 had been a productive year for Cather. As she corrected proofs of *One of Ours*, taught her classes at Bread Loaf, and transformed "The Blue Mesa" into "Tom Outland's Story," Cather was also working on a new novel. This one, her sixth, would be short—only 174 pages in the first edition—and its writing seemed effortless, in contrast to her labors on *My Ántonia* and *One of Ours*. She had finished the first draft before going to Red Cloud in November, and when she returned to New York in January 1923 she made final changes in the manuscript. She called her new book *A Lost Lady*.

Like her most recent novels, *A Lost Lady* focused on a single character who was based on a real figure in Cather's own life. However, in the case of both *My Ántonia* and *One of Ours*, Cather had worked intensively over several years to create a meaningful context for her central character. The message that these novels express came from an elaborate and painstaking interweaving of her leading characters with their settings.

A Lost Lady, by contrast, is a simply told tale, almost like a fable. From the outset Cather knew what she wanted to say and how she wanted to say it; the real-life figures on whom her characters were based gave her the story she wished to tell, from beginning to end. Annie Pavelka and G.P. Cather had been ideas around which she constructed stories. But in Lyra

Garber, the real-life Marian Forrester of *A Lost Lady*, Cather found a ready-made story, with little need for invention and expansion.

Such a story lent itself well to the succinct, spare writing style of the author she admired most, Gustave Flaubert. Since adolescence Cather had looked up to Flaubert as a master, but for many years she had more often imitated the very different style of the American novelist Henry James. Where Flaubert was concise, fashioning his stories from brief, exact, objective observations, James was discursive, offering lengthy, descriptive paragraphs of elaborately constructed sentences.

It was Sarah Orne Jewett who had redirected Cather, gently urging her to develop her own style, but all five of her novels to date had exhibited signs of James's influence in varying degrees. By 1922, a decade after becoming a published novelist, Cather had at last worked out a set of literary principles for herself to follow, based on the precepts of Flaubert, and *A Lost Lady* was her first book that meticulously observed those principles.

In April 1922, while working on her sixth novel, Cather published an essay about writing in an American magazine, *The New Republic*. Called "The Novel Démeublé" (*démeublé* is a French word meaning "unfurnished"), the essay called for an end to "overfurnished" novels—novels with too many irrelevant details. Simplification, not accumulation, should become the novelist's guiding principle, she said.

"Whatever is felt upon the page without being specifically named there—that, one might say, is created," Cather wrote. "It is the inexplicable presence of the thing not named, of the overtone divined by the ear but not heard by it, the verbal mood, the emotional aura of the fact or the thing or the deed, that gives high quality to the novel or the drama, as well as to poetry itself."[4]

Cather had been inspired to write *A Lost Lady* in the spring of 1921, after learning of the death of Lyra Garber. Cather had many childhood memories of the elegant Mrs. Garber, whose husband, Silas Garber, had been a founder of Red Cloud and later served as governor of Nebraska. In her novel, she used a

male narrator named Niel Herbert to tell the story of Lyra Gar-
ber/Marian Forrester over a period of several decades. Like Jim
Burden, the narrator of *My Ántonia*, Niel has a childhood similar to Cather's while growing up in the town of Sweet Water,
still another fictional re-creation of Red Cloud.

A Lost Lady has no real plot. Instead, it depicts the social
and physical decline of Marian Forrester, a decline that parallels the degeneration of life on the prairie. In Part I of the
novel, Marian and her much-older husband, Captain Forrester,
are presented initially as the town's leading citizens, but as
Niel grows older he discovers cracks in the façade that they
present to the world. When a depression occurs that decreases
their financial resources, Marian begins an affair with a
younger man named Frank Ellinger. The Captain subsequently
loses his money and suffers a stroke, and Marian is forced to
assume the care of husband and household herself.

In Part II Marian turns to the unscrupulous young lawyer
Ivy Peters for financial advice as she struggles to maintain her
home. When Ellinger deserts her to marry a younger woman,
Marian has a series of affairs with other young men in the
town. Eventually Peters becomes her lover, too, spending more
and more time at the Forrester house after the Captain dies. In
Niel's eyes her alliance with the crude, money-hungry Peters
marks her final degradation.

The decline of the "lost lady" has a broader meaning as
well. Describing the attitude of Niel, now a college student in
the East, Cather writes:

> *The people, the very country itself, were changing so fast that
> there would be nothing to come back to. . . . He had seen the
> end of an era, the sunset of the pioneer. . . . This was the very
> end of the road-making of the West. . . . It was already gone,
> that age; nothing could ever bring it back. . . . It was what he
> most held against Mrs. Forrester; that she was not willing to
> immolate herself, . . . and die with the pioneer period to which
> she belonged; that she preferred life on any terms.*[5]

Years pass, and Niel settles permanently in New York.

Meanwhile, the greedy Peters takes over the farm and Marian returns to her native California, where she marries a wealthy Englishman and settles in South America. Here she reclaims some of her former elegance. Niel hears of her later life through a childhood friend, who also tells him of Marian Forrester's death. Despite his earlier feelings, Niel is relieved and happy to learn that "'she was well cared for, to the very end.'"[6] In the end, Cather seems to be telling her readers, surviving is a matter of compromise, no matter how distasteful it may seem.

A Lost Lady was serialized in the *Century* in the spring of 1923—Cather earned $2,000 from its sale to the magazine— and was published in book form the following September. It sold well and received praise from leading critics. Other writers expressed admiration, too, including F. Scott Fitzgerald, who was working on the novel he would publish two years later as *The Great Gatsby*.

In 1923 Knopf also issued a new edition of Cather's poetry, under the title *April Twilights and Other Poems*. The young publisher aggressively promoted Cather's works and even sold movie rights to *A Lost Lady*. It was first made into a silent film that premiered in Red Cloud in January 1925; nine years later it was remade as a "talkie" with actress Barbara Stanwyck playing the part of Marian Forrester.

Cather was not especially impressed with the silent-film version of her novel, and she was outraged by the "talkie," which she felt misrepresented both her story and her characters. As a result, she wrote into her will a ban against future dramatizations of her work. The ban was respected until the early 1980s, when her short story "Paul's Case" was made into a television drama. In the early 1990s, two dramatized versions of *O Pioneers!*, one with music, were televised. No one, however, has yet dared make another adaptation of *A Lost Lady*, which critics today consider a masterpiece.

TWELVE

Many Journeys

In December 1923, when Willa Cather celebrated her fiftieth birthday, she could look back on the year with satisfaction. The Pulitzer Prize, financial independence, and the consolation of religion were now hers. The emotional anxieties that had reached a peak in 1922 seemed to have lessened. Added to them, however, were various physical ailments that would only increase as she grew older and would limit her activity as an artist.

In fact, Cather had written little during 1923 as she struggled with colds, chronic appendicitis, influenza, and neuritis in her right arm and shoulder. She spent seven months that year—from early spring until late fall—in France, much of that time with Isabelle McClung Hambourg.

Following lengthy treatments for her neuritis at the French spa city of Aix-les-Bains, Cather felt well enough to resume writing back in New York City in the winter of 1923–1924. She had decided to use the still unpublished "Tom Outland's Story," which she had finished in the summer of 1922, as the centerpiece for her seventh novel.

At her Bank Street apartment, Cather managed to keep to a daily writing schedule despite other commitments and distractions. Much to her dismay, she was now a celebrity and

By 1924, the year that celebrity photographer Nicholas Muray made this portrait, Cather had become one of America's leading writers.

received hundreds of letters, requests for interviews, and offers of speaking engagements. Cather, who valued her privacy, did not feel comfortable in the limelight. To handle the load of correspondence she hired a young woman named Sarah Bloom as her personal secretary, and Bloom remained with her for the rest of the writer's life.

One interruption that Cather welcomed was the chance to meet British novelist D. H. Lawrence, the celebrated author of *Sons and Lovers*, *The Rainbow*, and *Women in Love*. Lawrence and his wife, Frieda, stopped in New York City in March 1924 en route from the Far East to New Mexico. A mutual friend had suggested to Lawrence that he look up Cather, and the two writers enjoyed each other's company. Three months later, on her way to Red Cloud for a summer visit, Cather stopped in Ann Arbor to receive an honorary degree, her second, from the University of Michigan. During the next decade, Cather would receive five more honorary degrees—from Columbia, Yale, the University of California, Princeton, and Smith College.

Cather kept working on her new novel, which she had named *The Professor's House*, as she traveled to Grand Manan and Jaffrey before returning to New York. She completed the manuscript in January 1925 and submitted it to Knopf. As the book made its way through the production process, Cather turned to other projects. She wrote a preface to a collection of Sarah Orne Jewett's tales that she had compiled for Ferris Greenslet at Houghton Mifflin; the book was published later that year as *The Country of the Pointed Firs and Other Stories*. At the request of Alfred Knopf, she provided introductions to new editions of works by several authors, including Stephen Crane. She also wrote an essay on the British short story writer Katherine Mansfield, who had died two years earlier, for the company's annual magazine, *The Borzoi*. Cather admired both Crane and Mansfield, and she praised them for writing styles that adhered to the literary principles she had set forth in "The Novel Démeublé," her 1922 essay.

Cather's preface to *The Country of the Pointed Firs* is a revealing statement of Jewett's influence on the younger writer. Like "The Novel Démeublé," it is also a declaration of what Cather herself considered important in literary art. Several pronouncements in the preface are notable. The first is the quotation from Jewett's 1908 letter: "The thing that teases the mind over and over for years, and at last gets itself put down rightly on paper—whether little or great, it belongs to Literature."[1]

The second is Cather's own observation that if a writer

achieves anything noble, anything enduring, it must be by giving himself absolutely to his material. And this gift of sympathy is his great gift; is the fine thing in him that alone can make his work fine.[2]

Finally, there is this comment on Jewett's accomplishment:

She early learned to love her country for what it was. What is quite as important, she saw it as it was. She happened to

*have the right nature, the right temperament, to see it so—
and to understand by intuition the deeper meaning of all she
saw.*[3]

As appreciative critics would note after her death, Cather
embodied all these qualities in her own writing.

During this time Cather also wrote and published a long short
story, her first in five years: "Uncle Valentine." It appeared in
the magazine *Woman's Home Companion* in two installments in
1925. The story, set in Pittsburgh, focuses on a still youthful
composer named Valentine Ramsay—modeled after Cather's
friend Ethelbert Nevin—and describes his brief visit home after
years abroad, where he had gone to escape from an unhappy
marriage and to practice his art.

Back in Pittsburgh he is dismayed by the industrial expansion that has occurred in his absence, and by his discovery that
"the world belongs to what is rich and powerful, not to the
imagination and spirit,"[4] as one critic observes. He returns to his
mistress in France and a few years later is killed in an accident.

In the midst of this intensive schedule, Cather was also
writing a short work of fiction that would be published a year
later as her eighth novel: *My Mortal Enemy.*

Willa Cather enjoyed travel, and as her income grew the duration of her trips increased. Her journeys were not made to see
new places, however; instead Cather returned to the same
locales year after year, places that she valued and had come to
love. Her schedule now followed a predictable pattern: In the
spring and summer she traveled to the West and to Red Cloud,
and spent time on Grand Manan Island in Canada. Fall and
winter months were devoted to intensive writing in New
Hampshire and then New York City, interrupted sometimes by

a trip to Red Cloud during the holiday season.

Cather's journeys were not opportunities for leisure, for she hardly ever seemed to relax and do nothing; never did her brain go "off duty," and only during illness was she forced to give her body a brief rest. Sometimes on so-called vacations she continued work on the novel she happened to be writing at the time. Often she took along book galleys to correct. Even when she seemed only to be enjoying the sights, Cather was sensitive to the atmosphere of the places she was seeing, and she stored away her impressions for use in future books.

Cather's travels for 1925 began in May with a visit to Bowdoin College, in Brunswick, Maine. Cather was one of a number of leading American writers—including Robert Frost, his fellow poets Carl Sandburg and Edna St. Vincent Millay, and novelist John Dos Passos—who were invited to a centennial celebration of Bowdoin's Class of 1825. Nathaniel Hawthorne and Henry Wadsworth Longfellow had both been members of that class.

Cather spoke for nearly ninety minutes to a large, appreciative audience on the technique of the novel. Plot, she told them, was not important. As for characters, they had to be "born out of love, often out of some beautiful experience of the writer."[5] Atmosphere, she said, was the most important element; the author had to make his readers *feel* his setting. Not surprisingly, Cather was describing her own theory of composition.

In June Cather and Edith Lewis traveled west to the Grand Canyon in Arizona, then settled at a ranch in New Mexico while Cather corrected galleys for *The Professor's House*. In July they were on the road again, this time to Taos, near Santa Fe, New Mexico, where they were the guests of Mabel Dodge Luhan, a wealthy patron of the arts. Mabel's husband, a Native American named Tony Luhan, drove Cather and Lewis into remote mountain settlements in his prized Cadillac—a change from Cather's previous visit ten years earlier, when she traveled by horseback and wagon.

In addition to her interest in literature and painting, Mabel Dodge Luhan was also a leader in the growing movement to restore Pueblo Indian lands and villages to their original owners, and she tried to interest Cather in these efforts. Cather respected Native Americans and she was charmed by Tony Luhan, but politics never claimed her attention and she was never interested in any movements to improve society. Even when she worked at *McClure's*, she had managed to separate herself from the magazine's political and social crusades, concentrating instead on making its literary offerings first-rate. Art and politics, Cather believed, did not mix, and she strongly opposed the use of literature to promote reforms of society.

During her stay in Taos, Cather had another visit with D. H. Lawrence and his wife, then living on a ranch in the mountains nearby. Cather found Lawrence a friendly and entertaining host, and again she enjoyed his conversation. However, while acknowledging his giftedness, she never changed the judgment of his novels she had made in "The Novel Démeublé." His works were emotionally "overfurnished": he catalogued feelings in the same way that other "overfurnishers," like the nineteenth-century French novelist Honoré de Balzac, gave overly detailed descriptions of physical settings.

Leaving Taos, Cather and Lewis visited Santa Fe, then traveled on to Ácoma, an ancient Pueblo Indian village on a mesa west of Albuquerque. En route they passed the Enchanted Mesa, and Cather for the first time saw the legendary spot that she had heard about as a child and described in one of her earliest short stories, "The Enchanted Bluff."

Back in New York in September, Cather found herself in even more demand for speaking engagements. Propelling this renewed interest was critical and popular acclaim for *The Professor's House*. The novel had been serialized early that summer in *Collier's*—the magazine paid $10,000 for the right to print it—and published in book form several months later, during Cather's sojourn in the Southwest.

Willa Cather's seventh novel is set partly in southwestern Colorado and partly in the fictional midwestern college town of Hamilton, on the shores of Lake Michigan. But its figurative setting is within the mind and soul of Professor Godfrey St. Peter. Like Jim Burden and Niel Herbert, St. Peter is a version of Cather herself, but in *The Professor's House* he is not the narrator of another person's tale. It is his own life that is being examined, and thus Cather's life, too. In this novel Cather takes an inner journey as complex and meandering as her recent travels had been.

In Book I the reader learns that Professor St. Peter teaches history at the college in Hamilton. He specializes in the Spanish colonial period and is the author of a multivolume study, *The Spanish Adventurers in North America*. St. Peter has won a major award for this work, and his wife has used the prize money to have a new house built. But St. Peter does not want to move from the old house, where he spent many years writing his book and where the couple raised their two daughters, now grown and married. He is especially attached to his attic study and to the French garden he has created on the property.

Despite his success, the middle-aged St. Peter is dissatisfied with life. Today St. Peter's discontent would be diagnosed as a midlife crisis. Work that has kept him occupied for years is over, and he is depressed about the future. As an historian he observes that in the outside world traditional values have been replaced by materialism. Family life brings him no pleasure, either: he is estranged from one of his daughters because he dislikes her money-hungry husband, and his own marriage is unhappy. Added to his sorrow is the loss of his most promising student, Tom Outland, who was killed while serving in the army during World War I.

Book II of *The Professor's House* is "Tom Outland's Story," an account of Tom's life before he met the professor several decades earlier. Tom, a young railroad worker in the Southwest, discovers an ancient cliff city—similar to the one Cather had first seen in Mesa Verde ten years earlier. Fascinated, Tom and a friend excavate the site at Blue Mesa and collect artifacts, which they carefully catalogue. While Tom travels to Washington, D.C., in a vain attempt to interest the Smithsonian Institution in his discovery, his friend sells the artifacts. Sad and disillusioned, Tom lives for a while in the cliff dwellings. Here he is spiritually transformed and decides to educate himself. With money from his railroad job, Tom comes to Hamilton, where he meets Godfrey St. Peter.

In Book III Godfrey St. Peter is himself transformed. He stays behind in his old attic study while his family travels to Europe. One evening he lies down to take a nap and is nearly asphyxiated when a violent wind blows out the flame on his gas stove. He is rescued by the family's seamstress, who has come over to get keys to the new house.

Coming back to consciousness, St. Peter is aware that somehow he is a changed man. In his unconscious state "He had let something go—and it was gone: something very precious, that he could not consciously have relinquished, probably." He now feels that he will somehow be able to live "without joy, without passionate griefs."[6] In effect, he has accepted the inevitability of his death; he is no longer depressed by his mortality but recognizes it as the human condition.

Although she never openly acknowledged the connection, Godfrey St. Peter's turmoil and its resolution are Cather's own.

Cather interrupted her fall-winter working schedule in mid-November 1925 to travel to the Midwest, where she lectured on the modern novel at both the University of Chicago and the Women's City Club in Cleveland. By early December she was back in New York writing the book that would become her ninth novel; she had been questioned about it by reporters during her recent trip but had refused to say anything.

In March 1926 Cather's eighth novel, written quickly in the spring of 1925, was published in *McCall's* magazine; seven months later Knopf published it in book form. Entitled *My Mortal Enemy,* the work is the shortest of Cather's novels—only one hundred pages.

My Mortal Enemy is the story of Myra Henshawe, an orphaned Irish Catholic woman who is raised by a wealthy uncle. As a young girl she elopes from her small Midwest town to New York City with a man named Oswald Henshawe, a Protestant. Her family disinherits her, but Myra believes that her love for Henshawe will make her happy. In fact, their life together slowly deteriorates over the years. Henshawe fails in nearly every job he tries, and they are eventually reduced to living in poverty on the West Coast, where they have gone to make a new start. At the end of the story Myra, suffering from an incurable disease, dies, her dreams for happiness long since shattered.

My Mortal Enemy has been described as Cather's bleakest book—and at the same time praised as an almost perfect *novella,* or short novel. As an expression of her own midlife depression at its worst, the work offers little hope. Unlike *The Professor's House,* in which Godfrey St. Peter comes to terms with his life, *My Mortal Enemy* appears to offer no consolation to the reader.

On the other hand, rather than depicting hopelessness, Cather may have been presenting a variation of the theme expressed in *A Lost Lady:* unlike Marian Forrester, who learns to take life as it comes, Myra Henshawe allows her whole life to be destroyed by belief in an illusion—the illusion of romantic love.

Certainly Cather had given up her youthful illusions by 1926. "[W]hen you admitted that a thing was real, that was enough—now,"[7] she had written in *The Professor's House.* Like Godfrey St. Peter, she was now ready to carry on with life. Paradoxically, she would face the future by making an artistic journey into the historic past.

THIRTEEN

Death in the Southwest

Ever since Willa Cather's first visit to the American Southwest in 1912, the region had captured her imagination, and she found ways to introduce it into her fiction. She interwove memories of Walnut Canyon into *The Song of the Lark*, alluded to Spanish explorers in *My Ántonia*, and devoted a substantial part of *The Professor's House* to a fictional depiction of the discovery of Mesa Verde.

Cather believed, however, that the real history of the Southwest did not lie solely in the ruins of its ancient dwellers or in the explorations of Spanish adventurers. A major contribution to its past had been made by missionary priests from France in the nineteenth century, a fact that especially attracted Cather, a lifelong admirer of French culture. An accidental discovery made by Cather in the summer of 1925 gave her the focus and the incentive she needed to create her "Southwest novel."

The discovery had occurred in July of that year, when Cather and Edith Lewis stopped for a while in Santa Fe, New Mexico, en route from Taos to Ácoma. In Santa Fe Cather came across a rare book, *The Life of the Right Reverend Joseph P. Machebeuf*. It had been written by a priest named William Howlett and published in Pueblo, Colorado, in 1908. Joseph Machebeuf had been the first vicar general of the

Willa Cather, wearing her jade necklace, at the time she wrote Death
Comes for the Archbishop.

Roman Catholic Diocese of New Mexico upon its establish-
ment in the mid-nineteenth century. He had been a lifelong
friend and co-worker of Archbishop Jean-Baptiste Lamy, the
first Roman Catholic bishop of New Mexico. Cather had
known of Lamy for years and wanted to learn more about
him. She stayed up all night reading Howlett's biography of
Machebeuf, which included detailed information on the work
of Archbishop Lamy and the missionary priests.

Cather often said that the idea for writing her novels came
when an outside stimulus caused an "inner explosion" in her
mind.[1] Her reading of Howlett's biography created such an
"explosion," and she knew that she now had the subject for
her ninth novel. Another factor may have prepared the way
for this "explosion," too: Cather's religious faith. She was now

ready to write a book with a strong spiritual emphasis.

Cather began writing *Death Comes for the Archbishop* in September 1925 and had finished more than half of the manuscript by the end of April 1926, but she felt that she had to revisit the Southwest before its completion. In mid-May Cather and Lewis traveled by train to Gallup, New Mexico, and were driven to the Canyon de Chelly (pronounced "duh-*Shay*"), a site of cliff-dweller ruins in northeast Arizona and a center of Navajo culture. For the actual descent into the canyon, the two women made a pack trip on horseback.

After her trip to the canyon, Cather returned to her hotel in Santa Fe. For several weeks she wrote a few hours a day at the vacant home nearby of a writer friend named Mary Austin. There she completed the final chapters of *Death Comes for the Archbishop* before returning to New York in July.

Death Comes for the Archbishop began serialization in the magazine *Forum* in January 1927. During the next few months, Cather corrected galley proofs for the book, which was published by Knopf later that year.

Although Cather had written about the past in previous books and short stories, *Death Comes for the Archbishop* was her first work of historical fiction. The novel opens with a prologue, set in 1848 in Rome. Two priests, Father Jean Latour and Father Joseph Vaillant—her re-creations of Father Lamy and Father Machebeuf, respectively—are being sent by the Catholic Church to the New World. Latour is to become the first bishop of the newly created diocese of New Mexico and Vaillant, his friend, has been named vicar general. In the first section of the novel, Book I, Cather describes the arduous journey to the priests' new post, which includes a trip to Durango, Mexico, to secure their credentials.

In the next eight sections, or books, of the novel Cather recounts the missionary work of the priests from their arrival in Santa Fe in 1851 until the completion of the cathedral ten years later. Book IX, the book's concluding section, moves ahead several decades, to describe the last days and death of the archbishop. In a sense—and following traditional Christian belief—Latour's entire life has been a preparation for death, and the cathedral that he struggled so long to build becomes his final resting place.

Death Comes for the Archbishop is not a traditional novel, in the sense that it does not have a central plot. Cather, who believed that plot was unimportant and who valued instead the creation of atmosphere to *suggest* meaning, preferred to call the book a narrative. She likened it to a series of medieval frescoes (a *fresco* is a type of wall painting) that depicted scenes in the life of Geneviève, the patron saint of France; she had seen these frescoes in the Panthéon during her visit to Paris in 1902.[2]

Though Cather used Howlett's biography of Machebeuf as a major source, her novel focuses on the archbishop; his vicar general is of secondary importance. And while she follows the general outlines of Lamy's life in creating Jean Latour, she fictionalizes what she cannot know for certain about the actual archbishop's daily activities. Cather had read extensively about the settlement of the Southwest, and she interwove Latour's struggles with accounts of historical events in the region. She also included anecdotes and legends of Indians, Spaniards, and American settlers. Several historical figures make an appearance in the book under their real names, including the famous western scout and fur trapper Kit Carson.

Cather's familiarity with Roman Catholic doctrine and ritual and her sympathetic treatment of the Church won her praise from Catholic readers, most of whom assumed that she herself was Catholic. As the book became a best-seller, rumors spread that a dramatic religious conversion had caused her to write it. When she began receiving inquiring letters from readers, Cather decided to set the record straight.

In a long letter to the Catholic magazine *Commonweal*—which had carefully noted in its own favorable review of *Death Comes for the Archbishop* that Cather herself was not Catholic—she explained how she had been inspired to write the book and how she prepared for its creation, including talks with a Catholic priest in Red Cloud.[3]

Reviews of *Death Comes for the Archbishop* were almost uniformly positive. Critics seemed to appreciate the structure of the book and praised Cather for fashioning a masterpiece from the raw materials of history. As always, however, there were a handful of detractors, including some critics who protested that Cather had given too much credit to the French in the Southwest and had ignored the contributions of the Spanish. In her usual forthright style, Cather dismissed such complaints; as far as she was concerned, the real-life accomplishments of Archbishop Lamy and his associates spoke for themselves.

Cather's emotional state seemed strong in 1927, and her physical health was unusually good. Her living situation, however, was less than satisfactory. The construction of a new subway three doors from her Bank Street apartment had been going on for more than a year, and Cather was finding it increasingly difficult to work amid the noise and disorder.

By summertime Cather realized she had had enough and would have to move. After a long trip out west to visit family and friends, Cather and Lewis put their belongings in storage and moved out of the Bank Street apartment. They settled— temporarily, they thought—at the Grosvenor Hotel on lower Fifth Avenue, near their first apartment together on Washington Square. The two women hoped to find permanent lodgings during the following months, but their stay at the Grosvenor continued for five years. The precise reason why Cather lived as a transient for so long is not known. One explanation lies in the series of calamities that occurred in her life during these years.

Cather spent the winter of 1927–1928 in Red Cloud and stayed there until the end of February. In early March 1928, a week after she returned to New York City, her father died suddenly from a heart attack. He had had a mild attack the previous summer during her visit but had seemed to recover. A grieving Cather returned immediately to Red Cloud by train. She stayed for more than a month after the funeral, trying to come to terms with the loss while she took charge of the household.

Cather had been very close to her father—much closer than to her mother. Her ability to portray kind, loving father figures in her fiction—even the Church "fathers" in *Death Comes for the Archbishop*—was a reflection of how much she revered him. For her mother Cather always felt respect; she told friends that while Jennie Cather had taken care of her children's bodies, she had never tried to tamper with their minds. But Charles Cather had always been the favorite parent of his eldest child.

As usual when she was under stress, Cather's illnesses resumed. On her way back east from Red Cloud in April, she stopped at the Mayo Clinic in Minnesota for several weeks for treatment of an undisclosed ailment. Shortly after she returned to the Grosvenor Hotel, she became ill with flu and spent several weeks in bed.

Cather felt well enough by the end of June to travel to Grand Manan, where she hoped that the island's cool climate would restore her health. She was also looking forward to doing some writing, her first in many months. Cather and Lewis decided to travel to the island by way of Quebec, but their visit to Quebec City was extended when Lewis became ill. While Lewis recuperated in their hotel room, Cather explored the historic city, settled by French traders in the early seventeenth century. Although Quebec had been seized by the British in the eighteenth century, its architecture, language, and culture still reflected the city's French origins. Cather was delighted. In the evenings she settled herself in the hotel library and read histories of the city and of Quebec Province. The idea for her next novel had already "exploded" in her mind.

FOURTEEN

Shadows

When Cather and Lewis finally reached Grand Manan in late July 1928, a brand-new house welcomed them. Nearly two years earlier, Cather had bought five acres of wooded land near Whale Cove, overlooking the ocean, and had hired local workmen to build a small, two-bedroom cottage with an attic for her study. This was the first and only house that Cather ever owned. She furnished the cottage comfortably, but living conditions were rather primitive. It had no electricity or indoor plumbing; it also had no telephone, which pleased Cather immensely.

During her many summers on the island Cather kept to the same schedule. She worked after breakfast for several hours each morning, writing at a table in her attic study. As she had for years, she wrote her first drafts in longhand, then typed a revised version. (Cather kept a typewriter at the cottage for her use.) She made further corrections by hand before turning over the manuscript to her secretary in New York for retyping.

During her two months on Grand Manan in 1928, Cather's health gradually improved, and when she returned to New York in the fall she began writing her tenth novel. Her work was often interrupted in the following months, however, and she did not complete the novel until the end of 1930. Her primary concern during those years was the health of her mother, who suffered a stroke in late fall 1928 while staying at the home of Douglas Cather in Long Beach, California.

That Christmas, for the first time in many years, Cather did not return to Red Cloud. Several months later, in the spring of 1929, she traveled to California and for nearly three months helped her brother nurse Jennie Cather. Early in 1930 she returned for another long visit with her mother. Then Cather vacationed in France for several months and was reunited with Isabelle McClung Hambourg in Paris. During a visit to Aix-les-Bains that summer, Cather had a pleasant surprise: she met Mme. Caroline Grout, the elderly niece of Gustave Flaubert. Cather recorded the encounter in an essay, "A Chance Meeting," that was published in the *Atlantic Monthly* in 1933; it was later included in her book *Not Under Forty* (1936).

Cather worked on her French-Canadian novel intermittently, taking the manuscript with her on her travels to California and France as well as Jaffrey and Grand Manan. During these years she made four additional visits to Quebec City, determined to make the book as accurate as possible. One pleasant interruption in her writing occurred in the fall of 1930, when she received the prestigious Howells Medal, an award given every five years by the Academy of the National Institute of Arts and Letters, for *Death Comes for the Archbishop*.

At last, on December 26, 1930, in her room at the Grosvenor Hotel in New York City, Cather finished her novel. Entitled *Shadows on the Rock*, it was published in August 1931.

Cather's tenth novel is another work of historical fiction, set in Quebec in the 1690s. Like her previous novel, *Shadows on the Rock* has no plot; its six "books" recount ordinary events in the lives of a few of the 2,000 or so inhabitants of the city—situated on a "rock" in the St. Lawrence River—during a single year, when the French still control Quebec.

In a letter that was published after her death as an essay in

Willa Cather on Writing, the author described her impulse to write the book and incidentally explained the meaning of the title: "To me the rock of Quebec is not only a stronghold on which many strange figures have for a little time cast a shadow in the sun; it is the curious endurance of a kind of culture, narrow but definite." She intended to offer "a series of pictures remembered rather than experienced," and to depict an ordinary household that kept French culture "alive on that rock."[1]

The main characters in *Shadows on the Rock* are Euclide Auclair, a widower, apothecary (pharmacist), and loving father, and his twelve-year-old daughter Cecile, who is also his housekeeper. Along with the ordinary happenings that fill their days, Cather interweaves allusions to contemporary events and actual figures in Canadian and French history, including Bishop François Laval and Count Louis de Frontenac.

In a brief epilogue, the narrative moves ahead fifteen years. Cecile is now married and the mother of four sons, who will live in a new era of Canadian history. The golden age of King Louis XIV of France will soon come to an end, and during the lifetime of her sons the British will control the province of Quebec. But the "rock" of Quebec, a symbol of stability, will endure.

Cather's determination to write a book about French Canada puzzled some of her contemporaries. Many critics wondered why she had shifted her literary attention from the American West; they also wanted to know how she could have known so much about the region from five brief visits. These skeptics underestimated Cather's devotion to—and intimate knowledge of—French culture. They also failed to appreciate her ability to assimilate information as well as mood and nuance when she was captivated by a place or a person.

Not only did Cather read many histories of Quebec; she relied on a variety of sources for her careful depictions of domestic life. Her knowledge of French housekeeping, for example, came from her French cook, Josephine Bourda, whom she had been observing for years. Her ability to evoke the geographical setting was enhanced by her life on Grand

Manan, whose forests and coast resembled the landscape of
Quebec. Her familiarity with the practice and teachings of the
Roman Catholic Church, which Cather depicts as a powerful
force in sustaining tradition on "the rock," had been acquired
years earlier, when she had written *Death Comes for the Archbishop*.

Most of the reviews of *Shadows on the Rock* were favorable,
although both the critics and Cather herself realized that it
was less distinguished than its immediate predecessor. With its
affirmation of tradition and stability, the novel is the expression of an aging writer, as several critics have noted. It not only
advocates the maintenance of an established order; its very
writing, and Cather's necessary preoccupation with historical
"shadows," sustained her at a time when her personal life was
in upheaval. She was symbolically anchored by the "rock" of
Quebec for more than three years, from the moment when she
realized it would be the subject of her next novel to the final
correction of proofs. "I did the book to keep me going," Cather
wrote in a revealing letter to one reviewer, "and I'm well satisfied if a few old friends, like yourself, get a little happiness out
of it."[2]

Nineteen thirty-one marked the high point of Cather's popularity as a novelist. That year *Shadows on the Rock* was the most
widely read book in the United States. Cather was named one
of America's twelve most distinguished women by the magazine *Good Housekeeping*, and in August she appeared on the
cover of *Time* magazine. It was also a year of loss, however, for
Jennie Cather died in September in California.

By 1932 the United States and much of the world were
plunged in a deep financial depression that had begun with the
collapse of the stock market in New York in October 1929.
Cather herself had no cause for alarm; although she had lost
some money in the Wall Street "crash," she continued to
receive large royalties from her books. But she was distressed

*In June 1931, Cather received an honorary doctorate from Princeton—the
first degree awarded to a woman by that university. Other honorees at the
ceremony included famed aviator Charles Lindbergh (left).*

by the suffering of friends and relatives who had not been so
fortunate, and she sent money to many of them as well as
clothing and other items. Among the families she helped were
the Pavelkas; Cather saved their farm from foreclosure by pay-
ing their property taxes.

In August, during Cather's annual visit to Grand Manan,
Knopf published *Obscure Destinies*, a collection of three short
stories that Cather had turned to as a diversion during the
writing of *Shadows on the Rock*. All three stories are set in
Nebraska and make use of childhood memories. Each of them
concerns people of humble origins and tells a simple tale of
their lives and eventual deaths. The title comes from a line in
Thomas Gray's well-known "Elegy Written in a Country
Church-Yard," in which the eighteenth-century British poet—a
longtime favorite of Cather's—asks the reader to respect the

lives of ordinary, uncelebrated people, with "their homely joys, and destiny obscure."

The first story, "Neighbor Rosicky," describes the life and death of a Bohemian farmer modeled after Annie Pavelka's husband. In some ways a sequel to *My Ántonia*, "Neighbor Rosicky" became one of Cather's most popular stories and has been anthologized many times.

Many critics consider the second story in the collection, "Old Mrs. Harris," to be the finest that Cather ever wrote. In reality a novella, "Old Mrs. Harris" focuses on a pioneer grandmother and her family. The title character was inspired by Cather's grandmother Rachel Boak; characters patterned after the Wieners and other adult friends from Cather's childhood also appear.

The final story in the collection, "Two Friends," is the shortest. It recounts the friendship and eventual parting—through a political disagreement—of two small-town businessmen who closely resemble figures from her youth in Red Cloud.

Nearly every review of *Obscure Destinies* was positive. Critics seemed relieved that Cather's latest work explored the familiar territory of her Nebraska childhood, and they singled out for praise her ability to make the reader feel deeply about the lives of ordinary Americans.

In December 1932 Cather and Edith Lewis moved to a large apartment at 570 Park Avenue. Cather was relieved to have a permanent home after five years of hotel living, and she spent several weeks unpacking belongings that had been in storage. Many of her friends were surprised by her choice, however: Park Avenue was a place associated with the rich and snobbish, and Cather seemed to them simple and unpretentious. In truth, Cather *was* unpretentious—but over the years she had developed a decided taste for small luxuries.

She ate well, traveled first-class, and stayed whenever possible in comfortable lodgings. Although her ordinary "working costume" was a plain cotton middy blouse and skirt, she bought many expensive, brightly colored (usually red or green) clothes for dressy occasions (including several fur coats). She was not ostentatious, however, and could never bring herself to buy expensive jewelry.

Cather's new apartment had thick walls and carpets to keep out noise from the street and from neighbors; for her this was its most valuable feature. It was also very dark, a fact that seemed to bother her friends but not Cather; its only windows faced the solid brick wall of the Colony Club next door. Elizabeth Shepley Sergeant said that the place seemed like a cave.[3] For Willa Cather, the apartment at 570 Park Avenue became a refuge. As she grew older and her health declined, she was grateful for its protective comforts.

FIFTEEN

Slowing Down

N ow settled in what she probably realized was her final home, Willa Cather seemed to accept advancing age. She was not old—she had turned fifty-nine in December 1932—but the preceding decade had taken its toll on her health and vitality. She had managed to recover from an intense depression only to have to face the loss of both parents within a short period.

Cather had attained her life's goal; amid years of personal upheaval she had become a celebrated literary artist. But she now looked, moved, and sounded like an elderly woman. Her hair, pulled back in a loose bun, was still mostly chestnut but it was beginning to gray, and her face bore lines of weariness. Photos of her taken in the early 1930s reveal a stocky, heavyset woman who seems to be trying to conceal herself under layers of loosely draped clothing. Her expression is frank and slightly sad. Even her bright blue eyes, which in her youth twinkled with zest for life, seem tired, as though they have seen quite enough of the world.

Most human beings gradually decrease their activities and narrow their interests as they grow older. For Cather the process had accelerated in her fifties. Now she adopted the outlook and habits of old age, including an increasing desire for seclusion. Cather's former habits of sociability receded. Withdrawing into her Park Avenue apartment, she chose her rare social engagements very carefully, and her circle of friends grew smaller.

Cather's life was not entirely bleak, however. One happy event for her at this time was the rediscovery of music, which now became a major source of pleasure. During the turmoil of the Grosvenor years Cather had virtually abandoned concert-going. Now, through Alfred Knopf and his wife, she was reintroduced to leading classical musicians and resumed her attendance at recitals. She also enjoyed listening to recordings on an expensive phonograph that had been a present from the Knopfs.

Cather's love of music—and of children—brought another pleasure into her life: an enduring friendship with the American violinist Yehudi Menuhin, then a celebrated child prodigy. Cather had been introduced to the Menuhin family by Jan and Isabelle Hambourg in Paris during her visit in the summer of 1930. She had been instantly captivated by the fourteen-year-old boy and his two younger sisters, Hephzibah and Yaltah. The Menuhin family was then living in New York City, and in the following years Cather was able to spend many happy hours with all three of the gifted children, who called her "Aunt Willa." The children joined Cather for long walks around the reservoir in Central Park—in the winter they all went sledding together—and in the evenings she came to their apartment to read and discuss Shakespeare's plays. Cather was an appreciative guest at Yehudi's recitals, where he was sometimes accompanied on the piano by Hephzibah, and his many recordings gave her continuing pleasure over the years.

Cather had not abandoned her literary career when she moved uptown, and her reawakened interest in music had already inspired a topic for another novel. But she found it difficult to establish and maintain a regular writing schedule during the early months of 1933. A major reason was exhaustion: Cather often felt tired, "deadly tired," as she wrote in her diary, and had to rest a great deal. She was noticeably fatigued at a New York ceremony in February, when she was presented with a French literary award, the Prix Femina Américain.

Despite weariness, Cather accepted an invitation to address a banquet sponsored by Princeton University and held at the Plaza Hotel in New York City on the evening of May 4. Her short speech, carried live nationwide on NBC Radio, briefly summarized the history of the novel from its beginnings in the eighteenth century and expressed faith that it would continue. One line stands out: "'Because of the past, we have hope for the future,'" Cather said, quoting an inscription she had once seen in Paris.[1]

Also that spring, Cather had several long conversations about her career with her old friend Dorothy Canfield Fisher, who was writing a long article on Cather for the *New York Herald Tribune*. Summarizing Cather's reflections during their talks, Fisher expressed the author's belief that "escape" was a common theme in her writing. Fisher herself advanced the theory that "the only real subject of all her books is the effect a new country . . . has on people transplanted to it from the old traditions of a stable, complex civilization."[2]

Cather seemed to have mixed feelings about the article when it was published in late May. Although Fisher had said nothing in her analysis of Cather's writing that she absolutely disagreed with, the novelist probably felt uncomfortable with the rather detailed biographical summary that was also included. Somehow the whole tone of the article suggested that she belonged to the past.

Health problems continued to plague Cather, but she kept on with her new novel throughout the following months. By November she had completed the first draft at the Shattuck Inn in Jaffrey, and in New York that winter she worked on revisions. Her writing was interrupted for several weeks in the spring of 1934, when she sprained a tendon in her left wrist and overworked her right hand as a consequence—which meant she could not hold a pen for many weeks. Although Cather eventually recovered from this episode, problems with her writing hand continued for the rest of her life.

Cather finally delivered the completed manuscript of her eleventh novel, *Lucy Gayheart*, to Knopf in July 1934, but it was not published until August of the following year. Most reviewers were positive about the book and its heroine, a young girl from the fictional prairie town of Hanover (still another version of Red Cloud) who goes to Chicago in search of a musical career. Their praise, however, may have been a disguised tribute to the aging author rather than to the book itself, for *Lucy Gayheart* is not considered one of Cather's best novels, and Cather herself acknowledged its lesser importance.

Although the name of its heroine—Gayheart—suggests happiness, the book is a bleak account of a girl who wants to be an artist but fails. Full of romantic dreams, Lucy yearns to become a famous concert pianist and goes to Chicago in the late 1890s to study music. During the next few years she makes little progress musically but does manage to become embroiled in a relationship with a married singer named Clement Sebastian. Still clinging to her unrealistic career dream, she passes up the chance for marriage to a childhood friend, the attractive, prosperous Harry Gordon, because she cannot bear the thought of living out her life in tiny Haverford.

Lucy's tragedy is her inability to recognize and accept reality and her own limitations. Sebastian rejects her for his longtime accompanist, James Mockford, and the two men flee to Europe, where they drown in a sailing accident in Italy. Not long afterward, Lucy, still persisting in her desire to become a great musician, drowns while ice skating during a visit home to Haverford.

In 1935 several critics shared a common objection to *Lucy Gayheart*: the book and its subject were not relevant to the times, they said. Cather should have been writing about the Depression and the worsening political situation in Europe, they believed, and not the dreams and infatuations of a rather silly girl. Cather scoffed at that sort of criticism. Art, she continued to maintain, was not political and should never be used to advance a cause.

Although the charge of irrelevance is no longer heard, a major criticism leveled against *Lucy Gayheart* when it was first published is still expressed today: the novel is alternately melodramatic and saccharine. Both drownings are abrupt and convenient ways for the author to move her story along quickly, almost as though Cather is already tired of the book and wants to bring it to a quick end. Moreover, the tearful sentiments expressed by Harry Gordon as he laments Lucy's loss and his own misery (he has, predictably, married unhappily) seem excessive.

In the end, Cather does not make the reader care deeply enough about her heroine. In this relatively short work she does not present Lucy as a character for whom we can feel much sympathy. Readers may be more exasperated by Lucy than anything else. Yet that may be the very point that Cather wished to make, for *Lucy Gayheart* is much like the earlier *My Mortal Enemy* in its theme. Cather's message in both novels is the same: romantic dreams that have no basis in reality are doomed.

Although the character of Lucy was based in part on a girl whom Cather had known in Red Cloud, some critics have seen Cather herself in the portrait. They have concluded that Cather's darkest novels—*One of Ours, My Mortal Enemy, Lucy Gayheart*—express her own sense of failure. It is important, however, to separate Cather's personal life from the meaning of her fiction. After Cather left Red Cloud to find her place in "the kingdom of art," she made steady progress toward eventual recognition as a major literary artist. Along with enormous talent, she had the discipline and the willingness to work hard. By contrast, her failed heroines Myra and Lucy live on dreams—and are doomed as a consequence.

Cather certainly did not feel that she was a failure, although she may have been disappointed to realize that despite her success she would never achieve the legendary status of a Shakespeare or Chaucer. An acceptance of one's limitations—and recognition of what happens when such acceptance is not made—comes finally in maturity. *Lucy Gayheart* is imperfect as a work of art, but no one can deny that its message is one of wisdom.

The completion of *Lucy Gayheart* in July 1934 marked the beginning of a long period when Cather did no writing. She rested during the following fall and winter, attended concerts, and socialized with the Knopfs as well as the Menuhins and other prominent musicians. In the spring of 1935 she was ill again, this time with recurring bouts of appendicitis, and when she felt well enough to write again she was faced with a new difficulty.

Isabelle McClung Hambourg had returned to New York for medical treatment and was diagnosed with an incurable kidney ailment. While Jan toured the country, teaching and giving concerts to support the couple, Cather spent many hours each day at Isabelle's bedside. That fall, when the Hambourgs returned to Paris, Cather joined them there after a brief vacation in Italy. She left reluctantly in November, knowing that she had probably seen Isabelle for the last time, and spent another winter in New York without writing any new fiction.

Beginning in the spring of 1936, Cather had a new project to divert her. Ferris Greenslet had been interested for some time in having Houghton Mifflin publish a complete set of all her works. Although Houghton Mifflin was no longer her publisher, the Boston-based company still owned the rights to her first four novels. Moreover, the company published multivolume sets for other authors, a practice that Knopf did not follow. Cather brought up the matter with Knopf, and a financial arrangement was reached that allowed Houghton Mifflin the right to reprint the novels that his company owned.

For several years Cather occupied herself with the Autograph Edition, as the new printing was called. She went over each of the included works carefully—her novels, *April Twi-*

As she grew older, Cather disliked having her picture taken. She posed reluctantly in 1936 for a friend, the writer and photographer Carl Van Vechten, at the office of her publisher, Alfred Knopf, in New York City.

lights, and the story collection *Obscure Destinies*—and made many changes, most of them small cuts in the texts. Although Cather grumbled in letters to friends about all the bother the project was causing her, she was genuinely pleased with the outcome and was proud when the books started appearing toward the end of 1937.

During the 1930s, as the Depression worsened, a number of writers and other figures in the arts became political activists. In their art they depicted human suffering as a consequence of capitalism, an economic system based on free enterprise that underlies many Western democracies, including the United States. Many of these left-wing artists found much to admire in Communism, an alternative economic and political philosophy in which the needs of the group, rather than the rights of individuals, are stressed. Communism had appeared to succeed in the Soviet Union, and left-wing artists and their supporters believed that the Communist system should replace democratic government in America.

The voices of literary critics who were sympathetic to Communism were increasingly heard during the 1930s. They were, in fact, the major voices who praised works for their "relevance" and dismissed as unimportant any writing that did not support the cause of left-wing politics. Naturally Cather's works attracted their scorn, especially *Lucy Gayheart*.

About the time that negotiations were under way for the Autograph Edition, Cather decided to confront these critics head-on. In April 1936 she wrote a letter to the magazine *Commonweal*, answering publicly the criticism that her writing was "escapist"—diverting rather than politically relevant. (She was, of course, referring to the figurative meaning of escapist, although—as Dorothy Canfield Fisher had pointed out—Cather's works focused on literal escape, too.) Her art was deliberately apolitical, said Cather. As for the charge of "escapism," her letter asked, "What has art ever been but escape?"

One should not expect art to have "uses," Cather wrote, for all "true poets" are "useful" only to the extent that "they refresh and recharge the spirit of those who can read their language." Artists, she said, should pursue that goal rather than using their talents to reform society. Deploring the left-wing "revolt against individualism," Cather argued that artists can produce true art only if they are allowed to work as individuals and not as part of a political group.[3]

In the 1930s these sentiments were unfashionable, and among younger writers and critics Cather was increasingly dismissed as old-fashioned and conservative. Only many years later—long after her death—would her defense of artistic independence and her refutation of totalitarianism be admired instead of scorned.

SIXTEEN

Writing Again

Cather spent the summer of 1936 on Grand Manan, revising her books for the Autograph Edition, and she continued that work in Jaffrey during the fall. On Grand Manan she also assembled the six essays included in *Not Under Forty*, which Knopf published in November.

Sometime during the fall of 1936, Cather wrote a short story, her first attempt at fiction in several years. Called "The Old Beauty," it describes a once-beautiful woman and her eventual aging and death—familiar Cather territory. However, when she submitted it for publication to *Woman's Home Companion*, the magazine editor did not like the story and suggested that it was not up to Cather's usual high standards. Embarrassed, Cather quickly asked that it be returned. It was found among her papers after her death and published in book form with two other stories in 1948.

In the spring of 1937, Cather began her twelfth novel, *Sapphira and the Slave Girl*, a story set in Virginia in the nineteenth century. She worked on the manuscript at Grand Manan that summer and managed to make substantial headway, even though she had to devote considerable time to revisions and proof corrections for volumes in the Autograph Edition. In fact, for the next three years she would have to divide her time between writing the new novel and overseeing the Autograph Edition reprints of her previous work.

Back in New York that fall and winter, Cather continued to work steadily while resuming her limited social schedule of concert-going and visiting with close friends. In early spring 1938 she made a trip south to Virginia—her first since 1913—to see her ancestral home, Willow Shade. This was the setting for *Sapphira and the Slave Girl*, and Cather felt that she needed to reacquaint herself with the area before completing the book. The house itself was a disappointment; the present owner had cut down all the surrounding willow trees, and Cather decided not to go inside to discover what further changes had been made. But springtime in Virginia was as beautiful as she had remembered it from childhood, and the visit refreshed her.

Unfortunately, another dark period in Cather's life began soon after she returned to New York. One day in June her brother Douglas died suddenly of a heart attack in San Diego. Cather was so upset that she could not bring herself to return to Red Cloud for the funeral. She remained in New York that summer, despite the intense city heat, doing very little work. In October she received another blow: news of the death of Isabelle McClung Hambourg in Sorrento, Italy. Although Isabelle's death had long been expected, its actual occurrence was almost more than Cather could bear. Isabelle had been both dear friend and literary muse for nearly forty years. Many months later, describing her loss to a friend, the playwright Zoë Akins, Cather wrote that all of her books—not just *The Song of the Lark*, which bears McClung's name on the dedication page—had been written for Isabelle.[1]

During the winter of 1938–1939 Cather was further distressed as political events in Europe brought the world closer to war. Hitler's annexation of Czechoslovakia grieved her because of her longtime ties with the Pavelkas and other

Cather had this cottage built for her on Grand Manan Island, New Brunswick, Canada, in the mid-1920s. She summered on the island until World War II and wrote several books here, including her last novel, Sapphira and the Slave Girl.

Bohemians back in Nebraska. During the first six months of 1939 her emotional distress was matched by another series of illnesses. Only in June, after more than a year, was she able to resume work on *Sapphira and the Slave Girl.*

In early August Cather went back to her cottage on Grand Manan; she was still there in September, when World War II erupted in Europe. The war depressed Cather even more, and she buried herself in her writing in New York that fall and during the winter and spring of 1940. When her beloved France surrendered to the German army in June 1940, she mourned as if for a close friend.

Cather took the nearly completed manuscript of *Sapphira and the Slave Girl* to Grand Manan in August 1940 and finished it on the island that month. This would be Cather's last book published during her lifetime.

Although the exact moment of its origin is uncertain, Cather's intention to write *Sapphira and the Slave Girl* may have formed in her mind a decade or more before publication. Blanche Knopf knew about Cather's intention as early as 1931, for in a letter written that year she encouraged Cather to stop procrastinating and get started on her "Virginia book."[2] There is no record of what prompted Cather to begin writing *Sapphira* in the spring of 1937, but one explanation may be her desire to seek refuge from present turmoil in recollections of the past.

A central event in the plot of *Sapphira* comes from Cather's family history, and a scene reproduced in the novel's epilogue recounts an early childhood memory. One day in March 1879, when Cather was five years old, a former slave named Nancy Till returned to visit Willow Shade after an absence of twenty-five years. As a young woman, Cather's grandmother Rachel Boak had helped Nancy escape to Canada via the Underground Railroad. Now Nancy came to thank the woman who had saved her. As the fascinated child looked on, Nancy was then reunited with her own mother, Old Till.

Cather had first heard the story of Nancy Till's escape in infancy; her mother had even rocked her to sleep with a song about the escaped slave. Throughout her childhood, the story of Nancy Till was told over and over again, and Cather retained vivid memories throughout her life of the reunion scene, even details of the clothes that Nancy wore.

In *Sapphira and the Slave Girl*, Cather retells Nancy's story, relating imagined incidents that lead to the slave's escape. Most of the book is set in the year 1856 (a few years later than the actual event), on a prosperous farm in Back Creek Valley. Sapphira Colbert, the wife of a miller named Henry Colbert, has decided to sell her housemaid, Nancy Till, the illegitimate daughter of a white peddler and the Colberts' housekeeper slave Old Till. Her husband, who is kindhearted, opposes the sale and refuses to sign the documents. (Although the farm and its slaves are Sapphira's, under then-existing law the property of a married woman belonged to the husband.)

Sapphira, a cold, unlikable woman, schemes to get rid of Nancy by other means. Although the exact reason for her dislike of Nancy is never made clear, she obviously resents the humane way in which her husband treats the young woman. Slaves, Sapphira believes, are property, nothing more. Henry and the Colberts' widowed daughter, Rachel Blake, secretly thwart Sapphira's plan to have the slave raped. Finally, Rachel helps Nancy escape one night across the Potomac River, where she then proceeds northward to Canada.

Sapphira is predictably furious at her daughter's act and the two become estranged. A year later a diphtheria epidemic attacks the settlement in Back Creek Valley, and one of Rachel's daughters—Sapphira's granddaughter—dies. A reconciliation between the two women takes place, and a chastened Sapphira tells her husband, "We would all do better if we had our lives to live over again."[3]

Virtually every character in *Sapphira and the Slave Girl* is drawn from Cather's family and servants, most notably Nancy Till; Henry and Sapphira, who are Cather's maternal great-grandparents, Jacob and Ruhamah Seibert; Rachel Blake, who is her grandmother Rachel Seibert Boak; and Rachel's surviving daughter, Mary, who is Cather's own mother as a child. Enriching the main narrative are brief but engaging stories of other characters and their daily lives, many of which Cather recalled precisely from her childhood. Especially notable are Cather's memorable creations of black characters, none of which are stereotypes.

Sapphira and the Slave Girl is a story of good and evil, but its melodramatic moments do not overwhelm the narrative. There is enormous sadness in the book, but there is also humor and joy, as well as a sense of peacefulness and reconciliation in its conclusion. Cather had ended her writing career with a masterpiece that became a personal and public triumph.

The official publication date of *Sapphira and the Slave Girl* was December 7, 1940, Cather's sixty-seventh birthday. Its appearance capped a bittersweet year for the author. She had struggled to complete it as the shadow of world war hung over the United States. One year to the day, on her next birthday, her country would be drawn into the conflict when the Japanese attacked Pearl Harbor.

If Cather was nervous about public reaction to *Sapphira and the Slave Girl*, her concern was unnecessary. Readers loved the book; in a few short months some 250,000 copies were sold. Most critics were also full of praise and called it one of her best novels. Naturally Cather was pleased by this response, but there was little time to enjoy it. Signing a special printing of her novel, Cather injured her right hand and spent Christmas 1940 in New York City's French Hospital receiving treatments. As a consequence, a special brace was made for her; she had to wear it much of the time for the rest of her life.

Cather now sensed that the final decline had begun. Writing would be something she did with decreasing frequency. She felt battered—by the war, by life itself.

SEVENTEEN

"The End Is Nothing, the Road Is All"

U nable to write, Cather spent the first six months of 1941 resting, reading, and dictating letters to family and friends. Through newspaper accounts she followed major events of the war in Europe, including repeated German bombing attacks on England. In March the noted British novelist Virginia Woolf committed suicide, prompted in part by the bombings and their effect on her mental stability.

Cather was thoroughly sympathetic to the British cause at a time when many prominent Americans opposed sending aid to England because they feared it would draw the United States into the war. A lifelong Republican, Cather had nevertheless felt relief when Democratic Party candidate Franklin D. Roosevelt had been elected to a third term as President in November 1940. She had hoped that Roosevelt would do something to help the British, and she was pleased when he signed the Lend-Lease Act, granting Great Britain seven billion dollars' worth of military credit, in March 1941.

In June, despite her frail health, Cather made one last trip west by train to see her brother Roscoe, who now lived near San Francisco with his family, and returned east later that summer via Canada. Accompanying her as always was Edith Lewis. In all their years of living together, Lewis had managed their household, protected Cather from unwelcome intrusion, and made arrangements for their various moves and trips. With her arm constantly in a brace, Cather now needed help with the smallest personal tasks, including dressing herself, and Lewis was always there to assist her.

Cather's body was giving out, but her mind was still strong. Even before she could remove her hand brace for brief periods, she had decided to begin work on a new novel. Since her first trip abroad in 1902 with Isabelle McClung, Cather had been enchanted by the historic city of Avignon in southeastern France and had revisited it several times. She had long intended to write a novel about the city one day, and something—no one knows exactly what—reawakened that interest in the spring of 1941. Perhaps it was her concern over the fate of France in the war, and her desire to pay tribute to the country she loved nearly as much as her own.

During her western trip Cather read and reread a history of Avignon, and that fall she began making notes for the novel, a story of two boys set in the Middle Ages. During the next five and a half years Cather managed to write a substantial part of the novel despite her handicap, but she could never finish it. Following her instructions, Edith Lewis burned most of the manuscript soon after Cather's death. A perfectionist to the end, Cather had no intention of risking posthumous publication of a work she could not complete to her satisfaction.

During her remaining years Cather tried to remain active when her health permitted. She enjoyed the company of close friends and even entertained occasionally at her Park Avenue apartment. Yehudi Menuhin, who was now married, continued to be a special person in her life, and he visited Cather whenever he could.

Although she was past the age when new friends are normally acquired, Cather made an exception after she met the celebrated Norwegian novelist Sigrid Undset. The winner of the Nobel Prize for Literature in 1928, Undset had escaped with her son from German-occupied Norway and settled in New York, with the help of Undset's American publisher— Alfred Knopf. Undset had long admired Cather's work, and she asked Knopf to introduce her. Their friendship became a high point of Cather's last years.

The year 1942 brought more illness and gall bladder surgery. Once plump and robust looking, Cather now weighed a fragile 110 pounds. Prevented from returning to Grand Manan—because of wartime travel restrictions and concerns for safety—she and Lewis decided to spend the summer of 1943 in Northeast Harbor, Maine, on Mount Desert Island. The two women settled in a comfortable cottage near the Asticou Inn, which had a library stocked with the classics of English literature. Cather enjoyed rereading many old "friends" and for the first time read the entire works of Sir Walter Scott. She spent her last four summers at the Asticou Inn and never went back to Grand Manan; the trip was too arduous for someone in poor health, and she needed to be close to a hospital, should she need medical attention.

The war continued to hold Cather's attention, especially since family members and their friends were in military service. Many of them passed through New York and made a point of visiting Cather, which she found both agreeable and exhausting. The horrific destruction and loss of life continued to trouble her, and she referred often to it in her letters.

Although Cather had long opposed publishing her books in paperback, she relented during the war so that inexpensive editions could be made available to men and women in military service. She received many letters from soldiers telling her how much her books meant to them, and knowing that she had helped them in a difficult time meant a great deal to her. In her last years there were hundreds of letters to read from admirers around the world who enjoyed her books in translation.

In May 1944 a frail, white-haired Cather received a final award: the National Institute of Arts and Letters Gold Medal, given annually to a distinguished American novelist for lifetime

Cather rests her arm affectionately on the shoulder of old friend and former boss S. S. McClure following a ceremony at the National Institute of Arts and Letters in New York City in May 1944. Cather received the Institute's Gold Medal, its highest award, at the ceremony, which also honored McClure, novelist Theodore Dreiser, and singer and activist Paul Robeson (right). This is the last known photograph taken of Cather.

achievement. At the ceremony Cather joined several other prominent Americans who were receiving lesser awards: black singer Paul Robeson, whom she had met through the Knopfs, as well as novelist Theodore Dreiser and her former employer S. S. McClure, whom she had not seen in many years.

When Cather spotted McClure on the platform, she got up from her chair, walked across the stage to her old boss—now eighty-seven and even frailer than she was—and embraced him. The scene moved many in the audience to tears. A few weeks later, before going to Maine for the summer, Cather joined McClure for tea and they enjoyed reminiscing. It was their last visit together. McClure, who was sixteen years older than his protégée, survived her by two years.

At Northeast Harbor that summer Cather managed to write a short story, despite the limited use of her right hand. Entitled "Before Breakfast," it is set on Grand Manan and relates a brief moment of pleasure in the life of an aging businessman who has come to vacation on the island. During the fall of 1944 and into the following winter and spring, Cather worked off and on in New York on her Avignon novel, whose working title was "Hard Punishments."

Apart from an attack of flu, Cather's health was reasonably good. In the late summer of 1945, soon after the war ended, she and Lewis returned to Northeast Harbor. Here she wrote what would be her last short story, "The Best Years," about a young female teacher on the Divide at the turn of the century. Cather reached far back into her memories of childhood to create a major character in the story, another teacher named Evangeline Knightly. Miss Knightly is a fictional reconstruction of Cather's beloved Evangeline King.

Cather intended "The Best Years" as a special gift for her brother Roscoe, who had given up his dream of attending college and had taught school to help support the large Cather family. Soon after returning to New York, as she was preparing to send the story to Roscoe, a telegram arrived announcing that he had died following a heart attack in California.

Roscoe's death was heartbreaking for Cather, and any interest she had in continuing to write fiction dwindled away. That winter she grieved deeply. She spent most of 1946 in seclusion, seeing only her relatives and closest friends.

Gradually her distress receded and gave way to a profound calm. She read and reread Shakespeare's plays and poetry and the poetry of Chaucer. Music continued to be a major consolation, especially recordings that Yehudi Menuhin had made when he was very young. To her closest friends from childhood, Irene Miner Weisz and Carrie Miner Sherwood, she wrote long letters, reminiscing about the past and recalling what had pleased her most in her long career. She remembered again a line that had been her motto since university days, written by the French historian Jules Michelet (she had even inserted it in one of her favorite stories, "Old Mrs. Harris"): "The end is nothing, the road is all."[1] Her life was drawing to a close, and she was content.

Early on the morning of March 29, 1947, Willa Cather welcomed special visitors to her Park Avenue apartment. Yehudi Menuhin and his sister Hephzibah had brought his son and daughter and her two small sons to say good-bye, for all of them were sailing to Europe that very day. Several weeks earlier Cather had felt well enough to attend a concert at which Yehudi and Hephzibah played. Now, as another generation of young Menuhins sat respectfully in her drawing room, Cather recalled with fondness the many joys that this family had brought her.

The visit seemed to lift Cather's spirits. During the next few weeks she talked about writing again. In a letter to Dorothy Canfield Fisher she asked for memories of their visit to A. E. Housman in 1902; Cather planned an article on that memorable event. She began making summer plans and suggested to Lewis that they revisit the Southwest.

Cather slept late on Thursday, April 24, 1947. She awoke cheerful but still tired and decided to remain in bed. She had lunch brought to her at midday and then went back to sleep for several hours. Later that afternoon she awakened with a severe headache and summoned her secretary, Sarah Bloom. Not long afterward, at 4:30 p.m., Willa Cather died after suffering a cerebral hemorrhage.

The next day Willa Cather's obituary appeared in newspapers throughout the country, and within the next few days news of her death would be carried around the world. The headline in the *New York Times* on April 25 was typical—and so was the error it contained: "WILLA CATHER DIES; NOTED NOVEL-

IST, 70." Years earlier, Cather had listed 1876 as her year of birth in *Who's Who in America,* and the error had never been corrected. The correct date was not confirmed publicly until six years later, by Cather's first biographer, E. K. Brown.

After a private funeral service at her Park Avenue apartment, Cather's body was taken to Jaffrey Center, New Hampshire, for burial. Many years earlier Willa Cather had decided on Jaffrey as her final resting place.

Cather's surviving brothers, James and John, and several other relatives accompanied the casket to New Hampshire for a graveside service on April 28 conducted by an Episcopal priest. Later, a large white headstone was placed on the grave, with three separate texts carved on its surface.

At the top, WILLA CATHER is engraved in large letters. Below her name are the dates "December 7, 1876–April 24, 1947"—an error perpetuated by Edith Lewis when she accepted Cather's birth date in the *Who's Who* entry.

Beneath these dates is an inscribed tribute to Cather:

The truth and charity of her great spirit will live on in the work which is her enduring gift to her country and her people.

Finally, at the bottom of the tombstone are well-known lines from *My Ántonia:*

". . . that is happiness, to be dissolved into something complete and great."

Edith Lewis, Cather's principal heir, survived her friend by twenty-five years. After her death in 1972 she was buried at the foot of Willa Cather's grave; a small flat stone marks the spot.

EIGHTEEN

The Legacy of Willa Cather

At the time of her death in 1947, Willa Cather had published no new work in seven years, yet she was firmly established in the public mind as a leading writer. A year later, when Knopf published *The Old Beauty and Others,* a collection of her three last stories ("The Old Beauty," "Before Breakfast," and "The Best Years"), large sales reflected her undiminished popularity, and literary critics took the opportunity to write appraisals of her entire career.

Most of these appraisals were favorable; critics differed only on Cather's place in American literature. A few diminished her stature by calling her a regional writer, but most of them believed that she had created an enduring art of national interest. In the latter group was the *New York Times* critic Charles Poore, who wrote an appreciative review called "The Last Stories of Willa Cather," published in the *New York Times Book Review* on September 12, 1948.

In his succinct, full-page essay, Poore expressed a belief that later critics have confirmed—and readers have always known: Willa Cather is a major American writer. All of her works, he wrote, share a common theme: what the early twentieth century Spanish philosopher Miguel Unamuno called "the tragic sense of life," a characteristic of all great literature. Alluding to a notable passage from "The Novel Démeublé," Poore praised Cather for being able to write so that "something is felt on a page without being specifically named there."[1]

In the nearly five decades that have passed since Cather's death, her popularity has never diminished. All of her books remain in print and continue to sell a large number of copies. New collections of Cather's essays, newspaper reviews, and short stories have been published, and she has been the subject of at least a dozen biographies, both popular and scholarly.

Hundreds of articles on Cather's writing have appeared in academic journals, and critical estimation of her importance in American literary history continues to increase. One indication of Cather's prestige is her inclusion as the only woman profiled in *Sixteen Modern American Authors,* a highly regarded survey of research and criticism by Jackson R. Bryer that was first published in 1969, revised in 1973, and updated in a second volume in 1989. The amount of critical attention devoted to Cather's work has also increased as a result of the growing interest in women's writing since the 1970s.

Scholarly articles about Cather's work have focused on every imaginable subject. The most frequently discussed include Cather's seemingly contradictory love for both the Nebraska prairie and European-influenced high culture, the uses of music and religion in her fiction, and—what is considered Cather's single failing as an artist—her inability to portray positive, convincing relationships, both emotional and physical, between men and women. Many critics believe that this is a consequence of Cather's alleged difficulty with her own sexual identity.

Since the early 1980s, several feminist critics have described Cather as a lesbian and interpreted her writings from that viewpoint. This has provoked controversy, since many other critics are unwilling to categorize Cather as homosexual. As James Woodress, her most accurate biographer, has noted, there is no reliable evidence that Cather had a sexual relationship with anyone, including Isabelle McClung and Edith

Lewis. Moreover, Cather was a conservative woman, and this trait would have made her balk at any behavior that was judged unacceptable by contemporary social standards.

However, circumstantial evidence suggests that Cather was lesbian in *orientation*: at the University of Nebraska she had a passionate "crush" on her classmate Louise Pound; the person she loved most outside her family was Isabelle McClung; and she lived with another woman, Edith Lewis, for more than forty years. This orientation continues to be examined legitimately by critics for its influence on—and reflection in—Cather's work.

Cather was determined to preserve her privacy, and in her will she prohibited the publication of any of her letters. She tried to destroy as much of her correspondence as she could, and directed Edith Lewis to burn any letters uncovered after her death. Knowing her wishes, other friends of Cather's voluntarily destroyed her letters. Among them was Yehudi Menuhin's mother, Marutha, who had conducted an affectionate correspondence with the author over a number of years.

Nevertheless, some fifteen hundred letters of Cather's survive; most of them are in major libraries and are accessible to scholars. Despite Cather's prohibition against their publication, at least half a dozen have appeared in print, including several to Yehudi Menuhin, quoted in his autobiography, *Unfinished Journey* (1976).

In 1973, the hundredth anniversary of Cather's birth, the U.S. Postal Service issued a first-class postage stamp bearing her likeness—an honor reserved for the country's most prominent citizens. Traces of Willa Cather's life can also be found in many of the places where she lived:

In Gore, Virginia, a state historical marker identifies Willow Shade, Cather's first home; the house has been restored by a private owner but is not open to the public.

In Pittsburgh, the McClung house, where Cather lived, off

and on, for many years, still stands at 1180 Murray Hill Avenue. It is also privately owned and is not open to visitors.

A plaque at 5 Bank Street in New York City commemorates the site of Cather's longtime residence; the original building was torn down several years after she moved.

The buildings that housed Cather's second and last apartments in New York City—82 Washington Place and 570 Park Avenue, respectively—are still standing. So is the building at 35 Fifth Avenue, on the corner of East 10th Street, that was once the Grosvenor Hotel; a tablet notes Cather's residence there from 1927 to 1932.

The Shattuck Inn, Cather's retreat in Jaffrey, New Hampshire, closed during the 1940s and was used for many years by a Catholic religious order as a training seminary. Today the building is vacant and in disrepair; several efforts have been made to have it restored.

Untended for many years, Cather's home on Grand Manan Island, New Brunswick, was remodeled by one of Cather's nieces in the late 1960s and is maintained by family members as a private summer cottage.

Cather's last northeastern retreat, the Asticou Inn, in Northeast Harbor, Maine, is still in operation.

In the small town of Red Cloud, Nebraska, where Cather lived for over a decade, there are more than two dozen sites still in existence that were important in both her life and her fiction, including the Opera House and the building that housed Dr. Cook's Drug Store.

The Willa Cather Historical Center, a branch museum of the Nebraska State Historical Society, is housed in the former Farmers and Merchants Bank Building on Webster Street in Red Cloud; the bank was erected by Silas Garber, Cather's "Captain Forrester," in 1889. The Historical Center includes interpretive exhibits as well as an archive and library; a number of Cather's surviving letters and other documents relating to her life can be found there.

The Willa Cather Historical Center also maintains Cather's childhood home, two blocks away at 3rd Avenue and Cedar

Street. The residence was designated a National Landmark by the U.S. government in 1972. Visitors can see the house as it was when Cather lived there, including her attic room with its original wallpaper.

Both the bank building and the Cather home were restored by the Willa Cather Pioneer Memorial and Educational Foundation. Created to perpetuate both scholarly and popular interest in Cather, the Foundation sponsors an annual springtime conference on Cather's work that attracts participants of varied backgrounds from all over the country. In cooperation with the University of Nebraska/Lincoln, the Foundation also sponsors the International Cather Seminar, held from time to time in various Cather-related locations.

Willa Cather had a great love of nature. She was especially fond of trees—probably because they were so rare in Nebraska—and could never bear to see any cut down. She was an active supporter of the nationwide campaign for forest conservation in the early twentieth century and encouraged public celebration of Arbor Day, a holiday that originated in Nebraska in 1872.

One aspect of Willa Cather's writing that many readers find appealing today is the way in which it reflects her profound concern for the natural world and its preservation. Her writings include numerous descriptions of the countryside, in particular the prairie and its many wildflowers, and her greatest fictional villains are characters who wantonly despoil the landscape, like Ivy Peters in *A Lost Lady*.

Cather always discouraged any attempt to commemorate her life with any kind of monument; her books, she said, were her memorial. Her wish has been observed—with one exception that many believe Cather would have approved: in 1974 a conservation organization called the Nature Conservancy established the Willa Cather Memorial Prairie, a 610-acre tract of native tallgrass five miles south of Red Cloud.

NOTES

Chapter 1: Beginning a Journey

1. Willa Cather, in an interview printed in the *Omaha Bee,* October 29, 1921; reprinted in L. Brent Bohlke, ed., *Willa Cather in Person: Interviews, Speeches, and Letters* (Lincoln: University of Nebraska Press, 1986), pp. 31–32.
2. Willa Cather, in an interview printed in the *Philadelphia Record,* August 10, 1913; reprinted in Bohlke, ed., *Willa Cather in Person,* op. cit., p. 10.
3. Ibid.

Chapter 2: Red Cloud

1. Willa Cather, in a letter to the *Red Cloud Chief,* May 27, 1909; reprinted in Mildred Bennett, *The World of Willa Cather* (Lincoln: University of Nebraska Press, 1961), p. 257.
2. Bennett, op. cit., pp. 177–78. Cather's graduation speech is reprinted in *Willa Cather: A Literary Life,* by James Woodress (Lincoln: University of Nebraska Press, 1987), pp. 60–62.

Chapter 3: University Days

1. Excerpts from "The Opinions, Tastes and Fancies of Wm. Cather M.D." are reproduced in Bennett, op. cit., pp. 112–13.
2. "Concerning Thomas Carlyle," *Nebraska State Journal,* March 1, 1891, p. 14. Cather's essay is reprinted in *The Kingdom of Art: Willa Cather's First Principles and Critical Statements, 1893–1896,* edited by Bernice Slote (Lincoln: University of Nebraska Press, 1966), pp. 421–25.
3. Will Owen Jones, Editorial Note, *Nebraska State Journal,* November 1, 1921; quoted in *The Kingdom of Art,* op. cit., pp. 16–17.
4. Willa Cather, in *The World and the Parish: Willa*

Cather's Articles and Reviews, 1893–1902, edited by William M. Curtin (Lincoln: University of Nebraska Press, 1970), p. 274.

Chapter 4: Apprenticeship in Pittsburgh
  1. *Nebraska State Journal,* March 1, 1896, p. 9; quoted in *The Kingdom of Art,* op. cit., p. 417.

Chapter 5: Breaking New Ground
  1. "Prairie Dawn," *April Twilights* (1903; 1923; 1933), in Willa Cather, *Stories, Poems, and Other Writings* (New York: The Library of America, 1992), p. 788.
  2. Cather used Kingsley's lines as the second of two epigraphs in *The Troll Garden;* the first epigraph comes from a well-known poem, "Goblin Market," by the nineteenth-century English poet Christina Rossetti: "We must not look at Goblin men,/We must not buy their fruits;/Who knows upon what soil they fed/Their hungry thirsty roots?"
  3. "Paul's Case," *The Troll Garden* (1905), in Willa Cather, *Early Novels and Stories* (New York: The Library of America, 1987), p. 131.
  4. Cather's letter to her students is reprinted in *Chrysalis: Willa Cather in Pittsburgh, 1896–1906,* by Kathleen D. Byrne and Richard C. Snyder (Pittsburgh: Historical Society of Western Pennsylvania, 1982), p. 63.

Chapter 6: Making It in New York
  1. "148 Charles Street," *Not Under Forty* (1936), in Cather, *Stories, Poems, and Other Writings,* op. cit., p. 839.
  2. Ibid., p. 840.
  3. This version appears in "Miss Jewett," *Not Under Forty* (1936); in Cather, *Stories, Poems, and Other Writings,* op. cit., p. 854.

4. "The Enchanted Bluff" (1909), in Cather, *Stories, Poems, and Other Writings,* op. cit., p. 69.

5. Sarah Orne Jewett to Willa Cather, December 13, 1908, in *The Letters of Sarah Orne Jewett,* edited by Annie Fields (1911), pp. 247–50; quoted in "Miss Jewett," *Not Under Forty,* in Cather, *Stories, Poems, and Other Writings,* op. cit., p. 849.

Chapter 7: First Novel

1. *Alexander's Bridge* (1912), in Cather, *Stories, Poems, and Other Writings,* op. cit., p. 343.

2. Woodress, op. cit., p. 220.

Chapter 8: Harvesting the Past

1. *O Pioneers!* (1913), in Cather, *Early Novels and Stories,* op. cit., p. 170.

2. Quoted in "Miss Jewett," *Not Under Forty* (1936); in Cather, *Stories, Poems, and Other Writings,* op. cit., p. 849.

3. Preface, *The Song of the Lark,* 1932 edition. Reprint (Boston: Houghton Mifflin, 1983), i.

4. "Lost in Colorado Canyon," *New York Times,* August 26, 1915, p. 20.

5. *The Song of the Lark* (1915), in Cather, *Early Novels and Stories,* op. cit., p. 697.

6. Ibid., p. 685.

Chapter 9: The Triumph of Memory

1. Elizabeth Shepley Sergeant, *Willa Cather: A Memoir* (Philadelphia: J. B. Lippincott, 1953), p. 139.

2. *My Ántonia* (1918), in Cather, *Early Novels and Stories,* op. cit., p. 727.

3. Ibid., p. 937.

4. Ibid., p. 926.

5. Ibid., p. 918.

Chapter 10: Popular Acclaim

1. *One of Ours* (1922), in Cather, *Early Novels and Stories,* op. cit., p. 1258.

Chapter 11: A Search for Meaning

1. "Prefatory Note," *Not Under Forty* (1936), in Cather, *Stories, Poems, and Other Writings,* op. cit., p. 812.

2. *One of Ours* (1922), in Cather, *Early Novels and Stories,* op. cit., p. 1024.

3. Bennett, *The World of Willa Cather,* op. cit., p. 137.

4. "The Novel Démeublé," *Not Under Forty* (1936), in Cather, *Stories, Poems, and Other Writings,* op. cit., p. 837.

5. *A Lost Lady* (1923), in Willa Cather, *Later Novels* (New York: Library of America, 1990), p. 95.

6. Ibid., p. 98.

Chapter 12: Many Journeys

1. "Miss Jewett," *Not Under Forty* (1936); reprinted in Cather, *Stories, Poems, and Other Writings,* op. cit., p. 849. (Cather rewrote the Preface to *Country of the Pointed Firs* as an essay, "Miss Jewett," to include in *Not Under Forty.* The quotations cited here appear in both the original Preface and the later essay.)

2. Ibid., p. 850.

3. Ibid., p. 852.

4. Bernice Slote, in the Introduction to Slote, ed., *Uncle Valentine and Other Stories: Willa Cather's Uncollected Short Fiction, 1915–1929* (Lincoln: University of Nebraska Press, 1973), xxiv.

5. *Christian Science Monitor,* May 14, 1925; quoted in Woodress, op. cit., p. 362.

6. *The Professor's House* (1925), in Cather, *Later Novels,* op. cit., p. 271.

7. Ibid., p. 270.

Chapter 13: Death in the Southwest

1. Sergeant reports Cather's description of her cre-

ative process in *Willa Cather: A Memoir,* op. cit., p. 116.

2. "On *Death Comes for the Archbishop,*" *Commonweal,* November 23, 1927; reprinted in *Willa Cather on Writing* (1949) and in Cather, *Stories, Poems, and Other Writings,* op. cit., p. 960. Cather says here that she saw the frescoes "in my student days," but it is generally accepted that the encounter occurred in 1902, during her first trip abroad.

3. Ibid., pp. 958–62.

Chapter 14: Shadows

1. "On *Shadows on the Rock,*" *Saturday Evening Post,* October 17, 1931; reprinted in *Willa Cather on Writing* (1949) and in Cather, *Stories, Poems, and Other Writings,* op. cit., p. 966.

2. Willa Cather to the *Chicago Tribune* book critic Fanny Butcher (no date); quoted in Woodress, op. cit., p. 434.

3. Sergeant, *Willa Cather: A Memoir,* op. cit., p. 251.

Chapter 15: Slowing Down

1. *Princeton Alumni Weekly,* May 12, 1933; quoted in Woodress, op. cit., p. 451.

2. Dorothy Canfield Fisher, "Willa Cather," *New York Herald Tribune,* May 28, 1933; quoted in Woodress, op. cit., p. 452.

3. "Escapism," *Commonweal,* April 17, 1936; reprinted in *Willa Cather on Writing* (1949) and in Cather, *Stories, Poems, and Other Writings,* op. cit., pp. 968–73.

Chapter 16: Writing Again

1. Willa Cather to Zoë Akins, May 2, 1939; quoted in Woodress, op. cit., p. 479.

2. Blanche Knopf to Willa Cather, May 4, 1931; quoted in Woodress, op. cit., p. 481.

3. *Sapphira and the Slave Girl* (1940), in Cather, *Later Novels,* op. cit., p. 926.

Chapter 17: "The End Is Nothing, the Road Is All"
1. "Old Mrs. Harris," *Obscure Destinies* (1932), in Cather, *Stories, Poems, and Other Writings,* op. cit., p. 657.

Chapter 18: The Legacy of Willa Cather
1. Charles Poore, "The Last Stories of Willa Cather," *New York Times Book Review,* September 12, 1948, p. 3.

CHRONOLOGY

1873   Born Wilella Cather at her maternal grandmother's
        house in Back Creek Valley, Frederick County, near
        Winchester, Virginia, December 7.

1883   Moves with family to Webster County, Nebraska;
        lives at "Catherton," the family settlement on the
        Divide.

1884   Moves with family to Red Cloud.

1890   Graduates from high school; enters preparatory
        division, University of Nebraska, Lincoln.

1891   Cather's essay "The Personal Characteristics of
        Thomas Carlyle," published in the *Nebraska State
        Journal*, March 1, marking her formal debut as a
        writer.
        Enrolls as freshman at University of Nebraska in the
        fall.

1892   "Peter," Cather's first published short story, appears
        in *The Mahogany Tree*, a Boston magazine, in May.

1893   First drama review appears in *Nebraska State Journal*,
        Lincoln, November 5, beginning a nineteen-year
        career in journalism.

1895   Graduates from University of Nebraska.

1896   Moves to Pittsburgh to become editor of *Home
        Monthly*.

1897   Spends summer in Nebraska; returns to Pittsburgh
        and job as telegraph editor with *Pittsburgh Leader*.

1899   Meets Isabelle McClung in Pittsburgh.

1900   "Eric Hermannson's Soul," first Cather story to
        appear in a national magazine, published in
        Cosmopolitan, April.

1900–1901	Spends winter as a government translator and free-lance writer in Washington, D.C.
1901	Begins teaching at Central High School, Pittsburgh. Moves to McClung house; lives there until April 1906.
1903	Publishes first book, *April Twilights* (poems). Begins teaching English at Allegheny High School, Pittsburgh.
1905	Publishes *The Troll Garden* (short stories).
1906	Moves to New York City to work as an editor at *McClure's Magazine*.
1907–1908	Ghostwrites biography of Mary Baker Eddy for *McClure's Magazine*.
1908	Becomes managing editor of *McClure's Magazine*.
1911	Resigns as managing editor of *McClure's Magazine*.
1912	Houghton Mifflin publishes her first novel, *Alexander's Bridge*. Ends formal association with *McClure's*. Makes first trip to southwestern United States.
1913	Houghton Mifflin publishes *O Pioneers!* Ghostwrites autobiography of S. S. McClure.
1914	World War I begins in August; United States enters war in April 1917.
1915	Houghton Mifflin publishes *The Song of the Lark*. Visits Mesa Verde cliff dwellings (Colorado) and Taos, New Mexico.
1916	Isabelle McClung marries Jan Hambourg. Revisits Taos, New Mexico.

1917   Receives honorary doctorate, her first, from
        University of Nebraska.
        Visits Shattuck Inn, Jaffrey, New Hampshire, for the
        first time.

1918   Houghton Mifflin publishes *My Ántonia*.
        World War I ends with armistice on November 11.

1920   Begins long association with publisher Alfred A.
        Knopf.
        Knopf publishes *Youth and the Bright Medusa* (short
        stories).

1922   Knopf publishes *One of Ours*.
        First visit to Grand Manan Island, New Brunswick.

1923   Receives Pulitzer Prize for *One of Ours*.
        Knopf publishes *A Lost Lady*.
        Lives in France for seven months (April–November).

1924   Receives honorary doctorate from University of
        Michigan.

1925   Knopf publishes *The Professor's House*.
        Edits stories by Sarah Orne Jewett.
        Visits Southwest (Grand Canyon, Taos, Ácoma,
        Santa Fe).

1926   Knopf publishes *My Mortal Enemy*.
        Visits Southwest (Canyon de Chelly, Santa Fe).

1927   Knopf publishes *Death Comes for the Archbishop*.

1928   Receives honorary doctorate from Columbia
        University.
        Makes first visit to Quebec.

1929   Elected to membership in the National Institute of
        Arts and Letters.
        Receives honorary doctorate from Yale University.
        Decade-long Great Depression begins with financial
        collapse of Wall Street, October.

1930	Receives Howells Medal for Fiction from the American Academy of the National Institute of Arts and Letters for *Death Comes for the Archbishop*.
1931	Receives honorary doctorates from the University of California (Berkeley) and Princeton University. Knopf publishes *Shadows on the Rock*.
1932	Knopf publishes *Obscure Destinies* (short stories).
1933	Receives Prix Femina Américain; receives honorary doctorate from Smith College.
1935	Knopf publishes *Lucy Gayheart*.
1936	Knopf publishes *Not Under Forty* (essays).
1937	Houghton Mifflin begins publishing Autograph Edition of Cather's novels (1937–1941).
1938	Elected to membership in the Academy of the National Institute of Arts and Letters. Isabelle McClung Hambourg dies.
1939– 1945	World War II fought in Europe and Asia; United States enters war in 1941.
1940	Knopf publishes *Sapphira and the Slave Girl*.
1943	First visit to Asticou Inn, Northeast Harbor, Maine.
1944	Awarded National Institute of Arts and Letters Gold Medal.
1945	World War II ends, August.
1947	Willa Cather dies at her apartment at 570 Park Avenue, New York City, April 24; buried in Jaffrey Center, New Hampshire, April 28.
1948	Knopf publishes *The Old Beauty and Others*, Cather's last short stories.

FURTHER READING

I.   BOOKS BY WILLA CATHER

*The following books by Cather were published during her lifetime
and are listed in chronological order; unless otherwise indicated,
all are novels. The original date of publication is followed by
information on the most recent authorized edition of the individual
work.*

April Twilights. (Poems) 1903; 1923; 1933. Reprint (1903 ed.)
   Lincoln: University of Nebraska Press, 1990.

The Troll Garden. (Short stories) 1905. Reprint. Lincoln:
   University of Nebraska Press, 1983.

Alexander's Bridge. 1912. Reprint. Lincoln: University of
   Nebraska Press, 1977.

O Pioneers! 1913. Reprint. New York: Penguin, 1992.

The Song of the Lark. 1915. Reprint. Boston: Houghton
   Mifflin, 1988.

My Ántonia. 1918. Reprint. Boston: Houghton Mifflin, 1973.

Youth and the Bright Medusa. (Short stories) 1920. Reprint.
   New York: Random House, 1975.

One of Ours. 1922. Reprint. New York: Random House,
   1991.

A Lost Lady. 1923. Reprint. New York: Random House,
   1990.

The Professor's House. 1925. Reprint. New York: Random
   House, 1990.

My Mortal Enemy. 1926. Reprint. New York: Random
   House, 1990.

Death Comes for the Archbishop. 1927. Reprint. New York:
   Random House, 1990.

Shadows on the Rock. 1931. Reprint. New York: Random House, 1971.

Obscure Destinies. (Short stories) 1932. Reprint. New York: Random House, 1974.

Lucy Gayheart. 1935. Reprint. New York: Random House, 1976.

Not Under Forty. (Essays) 1936. Reprint. Lincoln: University of Nebraska Press, 1988.

Sapphira and the Slave Girl. 1940. Reprint. New York: Random House, 1975.

The following collections of Cather's writings were published after her death; these are listed in alphabetical order by title.

The Kingdom of Art: Willa Cather's First Principles and Critical Statements, edited by Bernice Slote. Lincoln: University of Nebraska Press, 1967.

The Old Beauty and Others. 1948. Reprint. New York: Random House, 1976.

Uncle Valentine and Other Stories: Willa Cather's Uncollected Short Fiction, 1915–1929, edited by Bernice Slote. Lincoln: University of Nebraska Press, 1972.

Willa Cather's Collected Short Fiction, 1892–1912, edited by Virginia Faulkner. 1965. Revised and reprinted. Lincoln: University of Nebraska Press, 1970.

Willa Cather in Europe: Her Own Story of the First Journey. 1956. Reprint. Lincoln: University of Nebraska Press, 1988. [Collection of travel articles written for the *Nebraska State Journal.*]

Willa Cather in Person: Interviews, Speeches, and Letters, edited by L. Brent Bohlke. Lincoln: University of Nebraska Press, 1986.

Willa Cather on Writing. 1949. Reprint. Lincoln: University of Nebraska Press, 1988. [Thirteen essays, including reprints of "The Novel Démeublé" and "Katherine Mansfield" from *Not Under Forty.*]

The World and the Parish: Willa Cather's Articles and Reviews, 1893–1902, edited by William M. Curtin. Lincoln: University of Nebraska Press, 1970.

Writings from Willa Cather's Campus Years, edited by James Shively. Lincoln: University of Nebraska Press, 1950. (Out of print)

Various reassembled collections of Cather's fiction have been published; the most accurate texts are available in the following Library of America editions of Cather's work:

Early Novels and Stories. Sharon O'Brien, ed. New York: Library of America, 1987. [Volume includes *The Troll Garden, O Pioneers!, The Song of the Lark, My Ántonia,* and *One of Ours.*]

Later Novels. Sharon O'Brien, ed. New York: Library of America, 1990. [Volume includes *A Lost Lady, The Professor's House, Death Comes for the Archbishop, Shadows on the Rock, Lucy Gayheart,* and *Sapphira and the Slave Girl.*]

Stories, Poems, and Other Writings. Sharon O'Brien, ed. New York: Library of America, 1992. [Volume includes Uncollected Stories, 1892–1929; *Alexander's Bridge; Youth and the Bright Medusa; My Mortal Enemy; Obscure Destinies; The Old Beauty and Others; April Twilights and Other Poems* (1933); *Not Under Forty;* and Selected Reviews and Essays, 1895–1940.]

II. SELECTED BIOGRAPHIES

At least a dozen book-length biographical studies of Cather have been written since her death. The most interesting are listed below; among them, James Woodress's biography is the most recent and the most comprehensive.

Bennett, Mildred. *The World of Willa Cather.* 1951. Revised and reprinted. Lincoln: University of Nebraska Press, 1961. [The first biography of Cather to appear after her death; includes interesting stories of her early life in Virginia and Nebraska. Illustrated. Note: Bennett's "revisions" for the 1961 edition include an index as well as endnotes that correct errors repeated in the text itself.]

Brown, E. K. *Willa Cather: A Critical Biography.* Completed by Leon Edel. 1953. Reprint. Lincoln: University of Nebraska Press, 1987. [First scholarly biography of Cather; critical evaluation of her work is useful, but biographical details are incomplete.]

Byrne, Kathleen D., and Richard C. Snyder. *Willa Cather in Pittsburgh, 1896–1906.* Pittsburgh: Historical Society of Western Pennsylvania, 1982. [Well-researched account of Cather's life in Pittsburgh. Illustrated.]

Lewis, Edith. *Willa Cather Living.* 1953. Reprint. Athens: Ohio University Press, 1989. [Lewis's biography of her friend grew out of notes she had made for E. K. Brown. Interesting firsthand account of Cather's interests and her reactions to books, events, and people.]

Sergeant, Elizabeth Shepley. *Willa Cather: A Memoir.* 1953. Reprint. Lincoln: University of Nebraska Press, 1963. [An absorbing account of Sergeant's longtime friendship with Cather, whom she first met at *McClure's Magazine* in 1910.]

Woodress, James. *Willa Cather: A Literary Life*. Lincoln: University of Nebraska Press, 1987. [Considered the most reliable biography of Cather. An objective, factual account of her life, with careful attention to detail; includes analyses of her major fiction, summaries of critical opinion, and numerous photographs. Replaces Woodress's earlier study, *Willa Cather: Her Life and Art* (1970).]

Woods, Lucia, and Bernice Slote. *Willa Cather: A Pictorial Memoir*. Lincoln: University of Nebraska Press, 1973. [Cather's life traced through photographs of herself, her family and friends, and her various homes.]

III. SELECTED CRITICAL STUDIES

Arnold, Marilyn. *Willa Cather's Short Fiction*. Athens: Ohio University Press, 1984.

Bloom, Edward A., and Lillian D. Bloom. *Willa Cather's Gift of Sympathy*. Carbondale: Southern Illinois University Press, 1962.

Giannone, Richard. *Music in Willa Cather's Fiction*. Lincoln: University of Nebraska Press, 1968.

Murphy, John, ed. *Critical Essays on Willa Cather*. Boston: G. K. Hall, 1984.

Randall, John H. III. *The Landscape and the Looking Glass: Willa Cather's Search for Value*. Boston: Houghton Mifflin, 1960.

Rosowski, Susan. *The Voyage Perilous: Willa Cather's Romanticism*. Lincoln: University of Nebraska Press, 1986.

Schroeter, James, ed. *Willa Cather and Her Critics*. Ithaca, N.Y.: Cornell University Press, 1967.

Slote, Bernice, and Virginia Faulkner, eds. *The Art of Willa Cather*. Lincoln: University of Nebraska Press, 1974.

Stouck, David. *Willa Cather's Imagination*. Lincoln: University of Nebraska Press, 1975.

IV. BIBLIOGRAPHY

Arnold, Marilyn. *Willa Cather: A Reference Guide*. Boston: G. K. Hall, 1986.

Crane, Joan. *Willa Cather: A Bibliography*. Lincoln: University of Nebraska Press, 1982.

Slote, Bernice. "Willa Cather." In *Sixteen Modern American Authors: A Survey of Research and Criticism*. Jackson Bryer, ed. 1969. Revised. Durham, N.C.: Duke University Press, 1973.

Woodress, James. "Willa Cather." In *Sixteen Modern American Authors, Vol. 2: A Survey of Research and Criticism Since 1972*. Jackson Bryer, ed. Durham, N.C.: Duke University Press, 1989.

V. MISCELLANY

March, John. *A Reader's Companion to the Fiction of Willa Cather*. Marilyn Arnold and Debra Lynn Thornton, eds. Westport, CT.: Greenwood Press, 1993. [An 880-page dictionary that includes thousands of entries on persons, places, artifacts, and quotations that appear in Cather's fiction; a guidebook to the sources of her art.]

INDEX

ACKNOWLEDGMENTS

The author wishes to thank Claire Quigley, director of interlibrary loan services at the Westport (Connecticut) Public Library, for her invaluable assistance. The author also extends her thanks to the following individuals: Helen Cather Southwick, Willa Cather's niece; Patricia K. Phillips, director, Willa Cather Pioneer Memorial and Educational Foundation, Red Cloud, Nebraska; Helen Mathew, director, Webster County (Nebraska) Historical Museum; Carl Esche, special collections assistant, Princeton University Archives; Lucia Woods Lindley; Martha Vestecka-Miller, Photographic Collections, Nebraska State Historical Society; Janice Madhu, International Museum of Photography at George Eastman House; Michele Fagin, Love Library, University of Nebraska; and Gilbert Pietrzak, Pennsylvania Department, Carnegie Library of Pittsburgh.

PHOTOGRAPH ACKNOWLEDGMENTS

Jacket and frontispiece by Edward Steichen, reprinted with permission of Joanna T. Steichen; facing p. 1 and on pp. 3, 9, 22, 25, 40, 49, 69, 89, and 98 courtesy Willa Cather Pioneer Memorial and Educational Foundation/Nebraska State Historical Society; p. 11 courtesy Lucia Woods © 1973; p. 16 courtesy Webster County (Nebraska) Historical Museum; p. 29 courtesy the Carnegie Library of Pittsburgh; p. 60 courtesy Helen Cather Southwick; p. 107 courtesy Princeton University Archives; p. 116 courtesy Carl Van Vechten Collection, Library of Congress; p. 120 courtesy Helen Cather Southwick; p. 127 courtesy Associated Press/Wide World Photos.